Better Homes and Gardens®
Mexican
cooking

Better Homes and Gardens® Books
Des Moines, Iowa

Better Homes and Gardens® Books
An imprint of Meredith® Books

Mexican Cooking
Editor: Jennifer Darling
Contributing Editor: Connie Hay
Recipe Writers: Marlene Brown, Linda J. Henry
Associate Art Director: Tom Wegner
Copy Chief: Angela K. Renkoski
Test Kitchen Director: Sharon Stilwell
Test Kitchen Product Supervisor: Dianna Nolin
Photographer: Mike Dieter
Cover Photographer: Mette Nielsen, Tony Kubat Photography
Food Stylists: Jennifer Peterson, Sue Finley (cover)
Photo and Prop Stylist: Nancy Wall Hopkins
Electronic Production Coordinator: Paula Forest
Editorial and Design Assistants: Judy Bailey, Jennifer Norris, Karen Schirm
Production Manager: Douglas M. Johnston
Prepress Coordinator: Marjorie J. Schenkelberg

Meredith® Books
Editor in Chief: James D. Blume
Managing Editor: Christopher Cavanaugh
Director, New Product Development: Ray Wolf
Vice President, General Manager: Jamie L. Martin

Better Homes and Gardens® **Magazine**
Editor in Chief: Jean LemMon
Executive Food Editor: Nancy Byal

Meredith Publishing Group
President, Publishing Group: Christopher M. Little
Vice President and Publishing Director: John P. Loughlin

Meredith Corporation
Chairman and Chief Executive Officer: Jack D. Rehm
President and Chief Operating Officer: William T. Kerr
Chairman of the Executive Committee: E.T. Meredith III

On the cover: Shredded Pork Tamales, page 44, and Oaxacan Rice and
  Beans, page 78
On page 1: Corn Tortillas, page 21, and Flour Tortillas, Spinach Tortillas,
and Chili Powder Tortillas, page 20

Our seal assures you that every recipe in *Mexican Cooking*
has been tested in the Better Homes and Gardens®
Test Kitchen. This means that each recipe is practical and
reliable, and meets our high standards of taste appeal.
We guarantee your satisfaction with this book for as long
as you own it.

Vibrant and colorful as a serape, Mexican cuisine is woven from the influences of the native peoples and Old World explorers. The country's diverse geography also led to distinct regional preferences that still characterize the cookery today.

In Better Homes and Gardens® Mexican Cooking, you'll find examples of many regional recipes, such as Puebla-style Chicken with Mole and Snapper Veracruz, and a few Tex-Mex favorites such as Chimichangas (check out our lower-fat baked version) and Fajitas.

Claire Rydell /The Picture Cube

Each recipe is introduced with a map that indicates the region with which the recipe is most closely associated. An accompanying anecdote offers a glimpse into the recipe's history or a tip about a special ingredient. To help you manage your time most wisely, most recipes include directions for preparing the dish ahead.

True Mexican cuisine is not just hot or spicy, but is sophisticated and complex. Let us be your guide as you explore the intriguing contrasts in Mexican food—soon you'll be a true aficionado.

Contents

CHILI PEPPER GLOSSARY 5

APPETIZERS AND BEVERAGES 6

BREADS 16

SALSAS 22

SALADS AND VEGETABLES 30

MEATS 38

POULTRY 50

FISH AND SEAFOOD 62

RICE, BEANS, AND EGGS 72

NUTRITION INFORMATION 85

DESSERTS 86

INDEX 94

METRIC INFORMATION 96

JALAPEÑO

CHIPOTLE

POBLANO

SERRANO

FRESNO

ANCHO

ANAHEIM

CHILI DE
ÁRBOL

CASCABEL

PEQUÍN

HABANERO

GUAJILLO

MULATO

YELLOW WAX

PASILLA

Chili Pepper Glossary

Though not all Mexican cuisine is spicy hot, many signature dishes get their distinctive flavors from the subtle variations in chili peppers. Rather than stinging the tongue, peppers are meant to stimulate the palate. Experiment with the array of fresh, dried, and pickled varieties to find those that match your own tolerance for heat.

MILD TO MEDIUM HOT

■ **Anaheim (ANN-uh-hime).** May also be named California. A large, long green pepper with a generally mild flavor. Often stuffed with cheese or chopped in salsas. Available canned as green chili peppers.
■ **Ancho (AHN-choh).** A dried poblano chili; reddish brown color. Available whole or powdered, it has a rich, slightly fruity flavor.
■ **Mulato (moo-LAH-toh).** A large, rectangular dried pepper with wrinkled, blackish brown skin. Medium hot; pungent.
■ **Poblano (po-BLAH-noh).** A large, fat deep green pepper good for stuffing. Flavor ranges from mild to medium hot. Available fresh and canned.

HOT

■ **Cascabel (KAHS-kuh-bell).** Small, globe-shaped dried peppers with reddish black skins. The seeds rattle inside. Nutty flavor, fairly hot.
■ **Chipotle (chih-POHT-lay).** Dried, smoked jalapeño peppers; dark reddish brown wrinkled skin. Flavor is sweet, smoky, hot. Also available canned, usually in adobo sauce.

■ **Fresno.** A waxy-type chili similar in shape to a jalapeño, but with a hotter, sweet flavor.
■ **Guajillo (gwah-HEE-yoh).** Medium-size, long, narrow dried peppers with smooth, dark reddish brown skins. Slightly smoky, hot.
■ **Jalapeño (hall-uh-PAIN-yoh).** Small with a blunt, tapered end. Can be green or red; medium hot to hot. Found fresh, canned, and pickled.
■ **Pasilla (paw-SEE-yah).** Medium-size, long, slender peppers with wrinkled, blackish brown skins. Pungent; medium hot to hot.
■ **Yellow wax.** Also known as Hungarian wax or banana peppers. Similar in size and shape to a jalapeño, with a waxy taste and hot flavor. Available fresh and pickled.

VERY HOT

■ **Chili de árbol (ARE-bowl).** Small, slender bright red pepper with smooth skin. Extremely hot, sharp flavor.
■ **Habanero (ah-bah-NEH-roh).** One of the hottest of all peppers; can be purchased fresh or dried. Also called Scotch Bonnet, they're small, bright orange, bell-shaped peppers. Add sparingly until you taste the dish—just one pepper will heat up a pot of chili.
■ **Pequín (pay-KEEN).** Tiny oval or round dried peppers with wrinkled orangish red skin. Stinging hot. Sometimes called tepín chili peppers.
■ **Serrano (suh-RAH-noh).** A small, slender fresh pepper with a hot to very hot flavor. Green skin turns red as pepper ripens; use either color interchangeably.

SHOPPING TIPS

Not all peppers are available at all times; like your favorite fruit, peppers may be sold fresh or dried, depending on the season. Look for peppers in Mexican or fresh produce markets and larger supermarkets. Select another pepper in the same heat category to substitute for one not currently available.

HANDLING WARNING

Because chili peppers contain very pungent oils (the membranes and seeds carry the heat), be sure to protect your hands when preparing either fresh or dried peppers. Put gloves or sandwich bags over your hands so your skin doesn't come in contact with the peppers. Always wash your hands and nails thoroughly in hot, soapy water after handling chili peppers.

USING DRIED CHILI PEPPERS

To prepare dried peppers, soften them in boiling water. Let them stand in the hot liquid until the skins become soft and pliable (about 45 to 60 minutes). Cut the peppers open and discard the stems, seeds, and membranes. Continue as your recipe directs.

TEMPERING THE HEAT

If the hot pepper you've sampled sets your tongue on fire, try drinking milk or cold beer. Dairy products and alcohol dissolve capsaicin, the hot oil that burns your taste buds. Or, foil the flames with rice, pasta, plain yogurt, or sour cream.

APPETIZERS AND BEVERAGES

REGION: NORTHERN MEXICO

Empanadas with Chicken Picadillo

EMPANADAS DE POLLO

MAKES 40 EMPANADAS   PREP: 1 HOUR   BAKE: 15 MINUTES

1 recipe Chicken Picadillo
3 cups all-purpose flour
¼ teaspoon salt
¾ cup shortening
1 beaten egg
½ cup milk
1 egg
1 tablespoon water

1. Prepare Chicken Picadillo; set aside.

2. For pastry, combine flour and salt. Cut in shortening until mixture resembles cornmeal. Add the beaten egg and milk; stir until combined. Turn out onto a lightly floured surface. Knead gently 10 to 12 strokes. Divide dough in half.

3. Roll out half of the dough into a 14-inch circle ⅛ inch thick. Cut into circles with a 3-inch round cutter. Reroll scraps to make 20 circles. Repeat with remaining dough.

4. Spoon about 1 rounded teaspoon of the Chicken Picadillo in center of each pastry circle. Moisten edges with water; fold in half, sealing edges with a fork. Prick pastry several times. Place on a greased baking sheet. Combine the egg and water; brush over pastry. Bake in a 425° oven for 15 to 18 minutes or until golden. Makes 40 empanadas.

CHICKEN PICADILLO

In a large skillet cook ½ cup finely chopped *onion* and 1 clove *garlic*, minced, in 1 tablespoon melted *margarine* or *butter* until onion is tender. Stir in 1 cup finely chopped cooked *chicken* or 1 cup *Shredded Savory Pork* (see recipe, page 45); 1 large *tomato*, peeled, seeded, and finely chopped (about 1 cup); ½ cup finely chopped, peeled *apple*; ¼ cup chopped *raisins*; 2 tablespoons finely chopped *pimiento-stuffed olives*; 2 tablespoons chopped *almonds*; 1½ teaspoons *vinegar*; ¼ teaspoon *ground cinnamon*; ¼ teaspoon *ground cumin*; and ¼ teaspoon *ground black pepper*. Cook, uncovered, over medium heat for 5 to 7 minutes or until apple is tender and mixture has thickened. Makes about 1¾ cups.

Empanadas are small pastry turnovers stuffed with sweet or savory fillings—in this case, picadillo. Picadillo is derived from the Spanish root picar, *to mince or chop. It refers to spiced, chopped meats, raisins, and nuts blended to produce a sweet and sour flavor. The result is a tasty snack of Old World inspiration. (See front in photograph on page 6.)*

NUTRITION FACTS PER EMPANADA		
		Daily Values
Calories	89	4%
Total fat	5 g	7%
Saturated fat	1 g	6%
Cholesterol	14 mg	4%
Sodium	34 mg	1%
Carbohydrate	8 g	2%
Fiber	.5 g	1%
Protein	3 g	

MAKE AHEAD

Prepare and bake empanadas as directed. Place in a freezer container or bag and freeze for up to 3 months. To serve, arrange the frozen empanadas on a baking sheet. Reheat in a 350° oven for 15 to 20 minutes or until heated through.

Front: *Empanadas with Chicken Picadillo (see recipe, above);* left, *Appetizer Tarts (see recipe, page 8)*

Sopes are popular appetizers throughout Mexico, although they may be called by other names, such as garnachas *or* chalupas, *in different regions. The edge of the corn-based dough is crimped to form a shell so it can hold a variety of savory fillings. (See left in photograph on page 6.)*

ALL MEXICO

Appetizer Tarts

SOPES

MAKES 24 TARTS   PREP: 1 HOUR   CHILL: 1 HOUR   FRY: 1 MINUTE PER TART

NUTRITION FACTS PER TART WITH CHICKEN FILLING

		Daily Values
Calories	98	4%
Total fat	6 g	9%
Saturated fat	1 g	6%
Cholesterol	16 mg	5%
Sodium	55 mg	2%
Carbohydrate	7 g	2%
Fiber	1 g	2%
Protein	4 g	

MAKE AHEAD

Prepare and bake tart shells as directed through Step 3. Place in a freezer container or bag and freeze for up to 3 months. To serve, arrange frozen tart shells on a baking sheet. Heat in a 350° oven for 8 to 10 minutes or until heated through. Fill as directed.

1½ cups masa harina tortilla flour
3 tablespoons all-purpose flour
½ teaspoon salt
½ cup water
1 beaten egg
¼ cup shortening, melted Cooking oil
1 recipe Chicken Filling or Black Bean and Cheese Filling

1. In a bowl combine tortilla flour, all-purpose flour, and salt. Stir in water and egg. Add shortening; mix well. Knead dough gently until moist but holds its shape. Cover and chill for 1 hour.

2. Divide the dough into 24 portions; cover dough to prevent from drying out. Roll each portion of dough into a ball. On a well-floured surface, pat each ball into a 3-inch round. Form a shell by crimping the edge of the round to make a ridge.

3. In a saucepan or deep skillet heat about ½ inch cooking oil to 365°. Fry shells 1 at a time, ridge side down, about 30 seconds on each side or until crisp. Remove tart shells with a slotted spoon. Drain tart shells upside down on paper towels.

4. Fill each tart shell with desired filling. If desired, place the filled tarts on a baking sheet. Heat in a 350° oven for 1 to 2 minutes or until heated through. Makes 24 tarts.

CHICKEN FILLING

Divide 1 cup finely shredded *lettuce* among tart shells. Divide 1⅓ cups shredded cooked *chicken* among tart shells. Top with a little *Ranchero Salsa* (see recipe, page 25). Makes enough filling for 24 tarts.

BLACK BEAN AND CHEESE FILLING

In a saucepan heat one 14½-ounce can *black beans*, rinsed and drained. Mash beans slightly with a potato masher or fork. Stir in ¼ cup desired *salsa*. Spoon hot bean mixture into tart shells. Sprinkle with ½ cup shredded *Monterey Jack cheese*. Makes enough filling for 24 tarts.

ALL MEXICO

Deviled Peanuts
CACAHUATES ENDIABLADOS

MAKES ABOUT 3 CUPS (24 SERVINGS)   PREP: 10 MINUTES   BAKE: 20 MINUTES

2 tablespoons margarine or
    butter
1 tablespoon lime juice or
    lemon juice
1 teaspoon ground cumin
1 teaspoon ground black
    pepper
½ to 1 teaspoon ground red
    pepper
¼ teaspoon salt
3 cups raw peanuts (1 pound)

1. In a saucepan combine margarine or butter, lime juice or lemon juice, cumin, black pepper, ground red pepper, and salt. Heat and stir until margarine or butter melts. Stir in peanuts; toss lightly to coat.

2. Spread peanuts in a 3-quart rectangular baking pan. Bake in a 350° oven about 20 minutes or until toasted, stirring occasionally. Cool before serving. Makes about 3 cups (24 servings).

DEVILED PEPITAS

Prepare as above, except substitute 3 cups *shelled raw pumpkin seeds (pepitas)* for the peanuts. Bake in a 350° oven about 15 minutes or until toasted, stirring occasionally.

Peanuts were used in Mexican cookery prior to the voyages of Columbus to the New World. A legume rather than a nut, the peanut is one of many foods introduced to the Old World. These spicy peanuts make a perfect snack to serve with before-dinner drinks such as margaritas, red wine punch, and Mexican beer. Pumpkin seeds, or pepitas, may be used instead of the peanuts.

NUTRITION FACTS PER SERVING		
		Daily Values
Calories	114	5%
Total fat	10 g	15%
Saturated fat	2 g	7%
Cholesterol	0 mg	0%
Sodium	38 mg	1%
Carbohydrate	3 g	1%
Fiber	1 g	5%
Protein	5 g	

MAKE AHEAD

Prepare and bake peanuts as directed. Place cooled peanuts in an airtight container and store at room temperature for up to 2 weeks or freeze for up to 6 months.

Rick Strange / The Picture Cube

Historically, quesadillas were turnovers made of corn tortilla dough, stuffed with cheese (queso in Spanish), and cooked on a comal, the traditional griddle. As a shortcut, today's versions use prepared flour or corn tortillas to enclose a variety of fillings. American-made Mexican cheeses are now available in supermarkets. Look for asadero, Chihuahua, or queso quesadilla for their superior melting qualities.

ALL MEXICO

Quesadillas

MAKES 12 SERVINGS   PREP: 20 MINUTES   COOK: 3 MINUTES PER BATCH

NUTRITION FACTS PER SERVING

		Daily Values
Calories	124	6%
Total fat	5 g	8%
Saturated fat	2 g	12%
Cholesterol	24 mg	7%
Sodium	238 mg	9%
Carbohydrate	11 g	3%
Fiber	0 g	0%
Protein	9 g	

1 medium fresh Anaheim pepper or one 4-ounce can diced green chili peppers, drained
1½ cups shredded asadero, Chihuahua, queso quesadilla, or Monterey Jack cheese
6 8-inch flour tortillas
1 cup shredded cooked chicken
½ cup chopped, seeded tomato (1 small)
3 tablespoons finely chopped green onions (2)
1 tablespoon snipped fresh cilantro, oregano, or basil
Guacamole (see recipe, page 22) (optional)
Fresh Tomato Salsa (see recipe, page 23) or salsa (optional)

1. If using Anaheim pepper, halve pepper lengthwise; remove seeds and membrane. Cut pepper into thin slivers.

2. Sprinkle ¼ cup of the cheese over half of each tortilla. Sprinkle pepper slivers or canned green chili peppers; chicken; tomato; green onions; and cilantro, oregano, or basil equally over cheese. Fold tortillas in half, pressing gently.

3. In a large skillet or on a griddle cook quesadillas, 2 at a time, over medium heat for 3 to 4 minutes or until lightly browned, turning once. Remove quesadillas from skillet and place on a baking sheet. Keep warm in a 300° oven. Repeat with remaining quesadillas.

4. To serve, cut quesadillas in half. If desired, serve with Guacamole and Fresh Tomato Salsa. Makes 12 servings.

Canned white beans are used as a base for this quick, high-protein, low-fat dip with Mexican flavors. Serve it with Tostaditas, or homemade tortilla chips, for a snack or appetizer.

ALL MEXICO

White Bean Dip
SALSA DE FRIJOLES CANARIOS

MAKES ABOUT 1¾ CUPS   START TO FINISH: 15 MINUTES

LOW-FAT

NUTRITION FACTS
PER TABLESPOON

		Daily Values
Calories	20	1%
Total fat	.6 g	0%
Saturated fat	0 g	0%
Cholesterol	0 mg	0%
Sodium	42 mg	1%
Carbohydrate	3 g	0%
Fiber	1 g	2%
Protein	1 g	

M AKE AHEAD

Prepare the dip as directed. Spoon into a storage container. Cover and chill for up to 3 days. Wrap and store the Tostaditas at room temperature for 4 days or freeze for up to 3 weeks.

DIP
3 **cloves garlic, minced**
2 **tablespoons thinly sliced**
   green onion (1)
1 **tablespoon olive oil**
1 **15-ounce can great northern**
   beans or cannellini beans,
   rinsed and drained
1 **4-ounce can diced green chili**
   peppers, drained
¼ **cup plain nonfat yogurt**
¼ **teaspoon salt**
¼ **teaspoon ground cumin**
¼ **teaspoon ground black**
   pepper
   Chopped tomato (optional)
   Sliced green onion (optional)

   Assorted vegetable dippers
1 **recipe Tostaditas or**
   purchased tortilla chips
   (optional)

1. In a small saucepan cook the garlic and the 2 tablespoons green onion in hot oil until tender. In a medium bowl mash beans and canned green chili peppers with a potato masher; stir in garlic mixture, yogurt, salt, cumin, and black pepper.

2. Spoon mixture into a serving dish. If desired, garnish with tomato and green onion. Serve dip with vegetables and, if desired, Tostaditas or purchased tortilla chips. Makes about 1¾ cups dip.

TOSTADITAS

Cut each of twelve 7- or 8-inch *flour tortillas* into 8 wedges. Spread one-third of the wedges in a single layer in a 15×10×1-inch baking pan. Bake in a 350° oven for 5 to 10 minutes or until dry and crisp. Repeat with remaining tortilla wedges, one-third at a time. Cool completely. Makes 96 chips.

ALL MEXICO

Cinnamon Hot Chocolate
CHOCOLATE CALIENTE CON CANELA

MAKES 4 (ABOUT 8-OUNCE) SERVINGS   PREP: 10 MINUTES   COOK: 10 MINUTES

3 ounces semisweet chocolate, cut up
1 tablespoon sugar
½ to 1 teaspoon ground cinnamon
4 cups milk
½ teaspoon vanilla
Few drops of almond extract
Whipped cream (optional)

1. In a blender container or food processor bowl, combine cut-up chocolate, sugar, and cinnamon. Cover and blend or process until finely ground.

2. In a large saucepan combine the ground chocolate mixture and milk. Cook and stir over low heat about 10 minutes or until chocolate melts. Remove saucepan from heat and stir in vanilla and almond extract. Beat with a rotary beater or Mexican molinillo until very frothy.

3. Serve in mugs. If desired, top each serving with whipped cream. Makes 4 (about 8-ounce) servings.

Chocolate enthusiasts insist the cacao bean was a richer New World "discovery" than the gold sought by the Conquistadors. When Cortez arrived in Mexico, Montezuma and his court enjoyed a beverage made from the ground cacao beans, water, spices, and honey. The Aztec emperor reportedly drank his xocoatl, *or bitter water, from golden goblets, which he threw into a lake after imbibing.*

NUTRITION FACTS PER SERVING		
		Daily Values
Calories	236	11%
Fat	11 g	17%
Saturated fat	7 g	35%
Cholesterol	18 mg	6%
Sodium	123 mg	5%
Carbohydrate	28 g	9%
Fiber	1 g	5%
Protein	10 g	

HOT CHOCOLATE THE EASY WAY

For convenience, Mexican homemakers purchase chocolate disks (far left) flavored with sugar, cinnamon, and/or ground almonds to prepare hot chocolate. The disks are broken into wedges and melted in hot milk before being beaten into a froth with the traditional molinillo, or carved wooden beater (near left). To create the froth, the molinillo is quickly rolled back and forth between the palms. Substitute a rotary beater, wire whip, or electric blender for similar results.

Ice cold margaritas long have been the cocktail of choice to sip with Mexican food. The tequila this drink is made with is a distilled spirit from the Agave tequilana plant, named for the town of Tequila near Guadalajara. Allow time for the lime to impart its flavor before mixing the margaritas.

NO-FAT

NUTRITION FACTS PER SERVING

		Daily Values
Calories	189	9%
Total fat	0 g	0%
Saturated fat	0 g	0%
Cholesterol	0 mg	0%
Sodium	3 mg	0%
Carbohydrate	22 g	7%
Fiber	0 g	0%
Protein	0 g	

ALL MEXICO

Margaritas

MAKES 6 (ABOUT 6-OUNCE) SERVINGS   PREP: 15 MINUTES   STAND: 30 TO 60 MINUTES

4 large limes
2 cups water
½ cup sugar
1 cup tequila
⅓ cup orange liqueur
1 cup ice cubes
     Lime wedges (optional)
     Coarse salt (optional)
     Crushed ice

1. Finely shred the peel from the 4 limes (you should have about 2 tablespoons). Stir lime peel into water. Let stand for 30 to 60 minutes. Strain lime peel mixture through a sieve; discard peel. Meanwhile, squeeze limes to make ½ cup juice; set aside.

2. Stir sugar into strained lime peel mixture until dissolved. Stir in reserved ½ cup lime juice, tequila, and orange liqueur. Pour into a blender container; add ice cubes. Cover; blend until ice is chopped. If desired, rub glass rims with lime wedges and dip in coarse salt. Serve over crushed ice. Makes 6 (about 6-ounce) servings.

Sangria probably was brought from Spain and adapted to Mexican ingredients when the Spanish began producing wine in the New World. The Mexican version uses orange and lime juices for a refreshing flavor.

NO-FAT

NUTRITION FACTS PER SERVING

		Daily Values
Calories	82	4%
Total fat	0 g	0%
Saturated fat	0 g	0%
Cholesterol	0 mg	0%
Sodium	46 mg	1%
Carbohydrate	9 g	3%
Fiber	0 g	0%
Protein	0 g	

ALL MEXICO

Sangria

MAKES 10 (ABOUT 4-OUNCE) SERVINGS   PREP: 10 MINUTES   CHILL: 3 TO 24 HOURS

1 cup orange juice
¼ cup lime juice
1 750-milliliter bottle dry
     red wine
¼ to ⅓ cup sugar
     Ice cubes
     Orange slices (optional)
     Lime slices (optional)

1. In a large glass or plastic pitcher stir together the orange juice and lime juice. Add wine and sugar, stirring until sugar dissolves. Cover and chill for 3 to 24 hours.

2. Serve over ice. If desired, garnish each serving with orange slices and lime slices. Makes 10 (about 4-ounce) servings.

ALL MEXICO

Jamaica Flower Water

AGUA DE JAMAICA

| MAKES ABOUT 6 (8-OUNCE) SERVINGS | PREP: 10 MINUTES | STAND: 30 MINUTES | CHILL: 4 HOURS |

6 cups water
1 cup loosely packed dried Jamaica or hibiscus flowers (1 ounce)
¾ cup sugar
2 tablespoons lime juice
Ice cubes

1. In a medium saucepan bring water to boiling. Remove from heat and add dried Jamaica or hibiscus flowers. Let stand 10 minutes. Add sugar, stirring until dissolved. Let stand 20 minutes more.

2. Strain flower mixture through a sieve, pressing flowers to extract as much liquid as possible; discard flowers. Stir in lime juice. Cover and chill 4 hours. Serve over ice. Makes about 6 (8-ounce) servings.

Jamaica flower water is a popular nonalcoholic drink found throughout Mexico. The dried blossoms of hibiscus flowers (above), *available in American health-food stores and Mexican groceries, are steeped to create a ruby red tisane or flower tea. Its refreshing taste is a nice alternative to carbonated beverages.*

J. Koontz / The Picture Cube

NO-FAT

NUTRITION FACTS PER SERVING

		Daily Values
Calories	98	4%
Total fat	0 g	0%
Saturated fat	0 g	0%
Cholesterol	0 mg	0%
Sodium	7 mg	0%
Carbohydrate	25 g	8%
Fiber	0 g	0%
Protein	0 g	

MAKE AHEAD

Prepare flower water as directed. Cover and chill for up to 3 days.

BREADS

ALL MEXICO

Spindle Rolls

BOLILLOS

MAKES 12 ROLLS   PREP: 45 MINUTES   RISE: 1½ HOURS   BAKE: 25 MINUTES

3¾ to 4¼ cups all-purpose flour
 1 package active dry yeast
 1 tablespoon sugar
 ¾ teaspoon salt
1½ cups warm water
    (120° to 130°)
    Cornmeal
 1 egg white
 1 tablespoon milk or water

1. In a large mixing bowl combine *1½ cups* of the flour, the yeast, sugar, and salt; add warm water. Beat with an electric mixer on low to medium speed for 30 seconds, scraping sides of bowl. Beat on high speed for 3 minutes. Using a wooden spoon, stir in as much of the remaining flour as you can.

2. Turn dough out onto a lightly floured surface. Knead in enough of the remaining flour to make a moderately stiff dough that is smooth and elastic (6 to 8 minutes total). Shape dough into a ball. Place in a lightly greased bowl, turning once to grease surface of dough. Cover and let rise in a warm place until double in size (about 1 hour).

3. Punch dough down. Turn dough out onto a lightly floured surface. Divide dough into 12 portions. Shape each portion into an oval about 5 inches long. Pull and twist ends slightly. Sprinkle cornmeal over 2 lightly greased baking sheets. Transfer rolls to baking sheets. Use a sharp knife to make a cut about ¼ inch deep down the center of each roll.

4. In a small bowl combine egg white and milk or water. Brush some of the egg white mixture over the tops and sides of rolls. Cover and let rise until nearly double in size (30 to 45 minutes).

5. Bake in a 375° oven for 15 minutes. Brush again with some of the egg white mixture. Continue baking about 10 minutes more or until golden brown. Remove rolls from baking sheets. Cool on wire racks. Makes 12 rolls.

Crusty rolls are found in bakeries (panaderías) throughout Mexico, a country renowned for its tortillas. Called bolillos, the rolls were popularized by the French during the brief reign of Maximilian in the 1860s. Now an integral part of the food culture, bolillo refers to the weaver's bobbin the rolls resemble. (See the photograph on page 16.)

NO-FAT

NUTRITION FACTS PER ROLL

		Daily Values
Calories	144	7%
Total fat	0 g	0%
Saturated fat	0 g	0%
Cholesterol	0 mg	0%
Sodium	140 mg	5%
Carbohydrate	30 g	9%
Fiber	1 g	4%
Protein	4g	

MAKE AHEAD

Prepare and bake rolls as directed. Cool completely. Place rolls in a freezer container or bag and freeze for up to 3 months. Before serving, thaw rolls at room temperature.

Front: Spindle Rolls (see recipe, above); upper left, Bread of the Dead (see recipe, page 18)

ALL MEXICO

Bread of the Dead

PAN DE MUERTO

MAKES 16 SERVINGS   PREP: 30 MINUTES   CHILL: 3 TO 24 HOURS   RISE: 1½ HOURS   BAKE: 35 MINUTES

The Days of the Dead celebrations honor deceased loved ones whose souls are believed to return during the first two days of November. At homes or in cemeteries, altars and gravestones are decorated with candles, fruit, strands of autumn marigolds, photographs of the departed, and portions of their favorite foods. Rich yeast breads, called pan de muerto, *are shaped into round loaves, decorated with dough in the shapes of skulls and crossbones, and sprinkled with sugar. Families visit the graves and feast together remembering happy times and reaffirming life after death. (See the photograph on page 16.)*

1 package active dry yeast
⅓ cup water (105° to 115°)
½ cup butter or margarine
¼ cup sugar
½ teaspoon salt
3 to 3¼ cups all-purpose flour
2 eggs
1 egg yolk
2 teaspoons finely shredded
   orange peel
1 teaspoon aniseed, crushed
1 egg white
2 teaspoons water
   Pink-colored sugar

1. In a large mixing bowl stir yeast into the ⅓ cup warm water. Let stand 5 to 10 minutes to soften.

2. Meanwhile, in a small saucepan heat butter or margarine, sugar, and salt just until warm (105° to 115 °). Add mixture to yeast along with *1 cup* of the flour, eggs, egg yolk, orange peel, and aniseed. Beat with an electric mixer on low to medium speed for 30 seconds, scraping sides of bowl constantly. Beat on high speed for 3 minutes. Using a wooden spoon, stir in as much of the remaining flour as you can. Cover and chill dough for 3 hours or overnight.

3. Turn dough out onto a lightly floured surface. Remove one-fourth of the dough; set aside. Shape remaining dough into a ball and place on a greased baking sheet. Flatten ball to 6 inches in diameter.

4. Divide reserved dough into 3 portions. Roll 2 of the portions into two 7-inch ropes to form crossbones. Combine egg white and the 2 teaspoons water. Place crossbones in an X on top of the loaf, attaching with some of the egg white mixture. Roll remaining portion into a 2-inch ball. Make a 2-inch-wide indentation in the center of the loaf; place the ball of dough in the depression, attaching with the egg white mixture.

5. Cover and let rise in a warm place until nearly double (1½ to 2 hours). Brush with egg white mixture and sprinkle with colored sugar. Bake in a 325° oven for 35 to 40 minutes or until done. Remove from baking sheet. Cool on a wire rack. Makes 1 loaf (16 servings).

NUTRITION FACTS PER SERVING

		Daily Values
Calories	160	7%
Total fat	7 g	10%
Saturated fat	4 g	19%
Cholesterol	55 mg	18%
Sodium	137 mg	5%
Carbohydrate	21 g	6%
Fiber	1 g	2%
Protein	4 g	

MAKE AHEAD

Prepare and bake bread as directed. Cool completely. Place bread in a freezer container or bag and freeze for up to 3 months. Before serving, thaw bread at room temperature.

ALL MEXICO

Three Kings' Bread
ROSCA DE REYES

MAKES 16 SERVINGS   PREP: 35 MINUTES   RISE: 1½ HOURS   BAKE: 30 MINUTES

DOUGH
3¼ to 3¾ cups all-purpose flour
1 package active dry yeast
⅔ cup milk
⅓ cup butter or margarine
⅓ cup granulated sugar
¼ teaspoon salt
2 eggs

FILLING
2 tablespoons butter or margarine, melted
2 tablespoons granulated sugar
½ teaspoon ground cinnamon
½ cup chopped almonds, toasted
½ cup diced mixed candied fruits and peels

ICING
1 cup sifted powdered sugar
¼ teaspoon vanilla
1 to 2 tablespoons milk

¼ cup sliced almonds
½ cup candied red and/or green cherries, halved

1. In a large bowl combine 1½ cups of the flour and the yeast; set aside. In a small saucepan heat and stir milk, the ⅓ cup butter or margarine, granulated sugar, and salt just until warm (120° to 130°) and butter almost melts. Add milk mixture to dry mixture along with eggs. Beat with an electric mixer on low to medium speed for 30 seconds, scraping the sides of bowl constantly. Beat on high speed for 3 minutes. Stir in as much remaining flour as you can.

2. Turn dough out onto a floured surface. Knead in enough remaining flour to make a moderately soft dough that is smooth and elastic (3 to 5 minutes total). Shape dough into a ball. Place in a lightly greased bowl, turning once to grease surface of dough. Cover; let rise in a warm place until double (1 to 1½ hours). Punch dough down. Turn dough out onto a floured surface. Cover and let rest 10 minutes. Roll dough into a 20×12-inch rectangle. Brush with the 2 tablespoons melted butter. Combine granulated sugar and cinnamon; add chopped almonds and candied fruits and peels, tossing to coat. Sprinkle over dough. Roll dough up, jelly-roll style, starting from a long side. Pinch seams to seal. Bring ends together to form a ring. Place dough, seam side down, on a greased baking sheet. Moisten and pinch ends together to seal. Flatten slightly. Use scissors to make cuts in dough at 1½-inch intervals around edge of ring, cutting two-thirds of the way to center. Cover; let rise until nearly double (30 to 40 minutes).

3. Bake in a 350° oven about 30 minutes or until bread sounds hollow when tapped (if necessary, cover loosely with foil the last 15 minutes of baking). Cool. For icing, combine powdered sugar and vanilla. Stir in enough milk to make icing easy to drizzle. Drizzle over bread; decorate with sliced almonds and candied cherries. Makes 16 servings.

Gifts are exchanged on January 6, or Twelfth Night, in Mexico, not on Christmas. This coincides with the day the Three Kings arrived in Bethlehem with gifts for the baby Jesus. During the festivities, a special yeast bread is served. Shaped in a ring and embellished with nuts and candied fruits, the bread resembles a crown. Inside, a tiny doll is hidden to represent the Holy Child. Depending on the age of the finder or family tradition, the person served the slice containing the doll is said to have good luck throughout the year or might be responsible for hosting the next party, on Candlemas, February 2.

NUTRITION FACTS PER SERVING		
		Daily Values
Calories	255	12%
Total fat	9 g	13%
Saturated fat	4 g	18%
Cholesterol	42 mg	13%
Sodium	101 mg	4%
Carbohydrate	40 g	13%
Fiber	1 g	5%
Protein	5 g	

MAKE AHEAD

Prepare, bake, and cool bread as directed; do not ice. Place bread in a freezer container or bag and freeze for up to 3 months. Before serving, thaw bread at room temperature. Ice and decorate as directed in recipe.

The Spanish brought wheat to the New World, giving rise to the evolution of flour tortillas in the wheat-growing region of Sonora in Northern Mexico. Lighter and more delicate than corn tortillas, a warm flour tortilla fresh from the griddle and smeared with butter is one of life's simple pleasures. Flavored variations of flour tortillas add interest to fajitas or chicken enchiladas.

REGION: NORTHERN MEXICO

ƒlour Tortillas

TORTILLAS DE HARINA

MAKES 12 (8-INCH) TORTILLAS   PREP: 45 MINUTES   COOK: 1 MINUTE PER TORTILLA

NUTRITION FACTS
PER 8-INCH TORTILLA

		Daily Values
Calories	89	4%
Total fat	2 g	3%
Saturated fat	1 g	2%
Cholesterol	0 mg	0%
Sodium	120 mg	4%
Carbohydrate	15 g	4%
Fiber	1 g	2%
Protein	2 g	

₥AKE AHEAD

Prepare tortillas as directed. Stack them, alternating each tortilla with 2 layers of waxed paper. Place tortillas in a freezer bag and freeze up to 6 months. Before serving, thaw at room temperature.

2 cups all-purpose flour
1 teaspoon baking powder
½ teaspoon salt
2 tablespoons shortening
½ cup warm water

1. In a medium mixing bowl combine flour, baking powder, and salt. Cut in shortening until combined. Gradually add warm water, tossing together until dough can be gathered into a ball (if necessary, add more *water,* 1 tablespoon at a time). Knead dough 15 to 20 times. Let dough rest for 15 minutes.

2. For 8-inch tortillas, divide dough into 12 equal portions; shape into balls. (For 10-inch tortillas, divide dough into 8 equal portions; shape into balls.)

3. On a lightly floured surface, use a rolling pin to flatten out each ball of dough into an 8-inch (or 10-inch) circle. Stack the rolled-out tortillas between 2 pieces of waxed paper.

4. Carefully peel off top sheet of waxed paper. Place tortilla, paper side up, on a medium-hot ungreased skillet or griddle. As tortilla begins to heat, carefully peel off remaining sheet of waxed paper. Cook tortilla about 30 seconds or until puffy. Turn and cook about 30 seconds more or until edges curl up slightly. Wrap tortillas in foil if using immediately. Makes 12 (8-inch) or 8 (10-inch) tortillas.

SPINACH TORTILLAS

Prepare as above, except add ⅓ cup very finely chopped, well-drained, cooked *spinach* with the flour.

CHILI POWDER TORTILLAS

Prepare as above, except add 1 tablespoon *ancho chili powder* or *chili powder* to the flour mixture (add more water, if necessary).

ALL MEXICO

Corn Tortillas
TORTILLAS DE MAIZ

MAKES 12 (6-INCH) TORTILLAS   PREP: 45 MINUTES   COOK: 2 MINUTES PER TORTILLA

2 cups masa harina tortilla
flour
¼ teaspoon salt
1¼ cups warm water

1. In a medium mixing bowl combine tortilla flour, salt, and water. Stir mixture together with your hands until dough is firm but moist (if necessary, add more *water*, 1 tablespoon at a time). Let dough rest for 15 minutes.

2. Divide dough into 12 equal portions; shape into balls. Using a tortilla press or a rolling pin, flatten out each ball of dough between 2 pieces of waxed paper into a 6-inch circle.

3. Carefully peel off top sheet of waxed paper. Place tortilla, paper side up, on a medium-hot ungreased skillet or griddle. As tortilla begins to heat, carefully peel off remaining sheet of waxed paper. Cook, turning occasionally, for 2 to 2½ minutes or until tortilla is dry and light brown (tortilla should still be soft). Wrap tortillas in foil if using immediately. Makes 12 (6-inch) tortillas.

The corn tortilla is the staff of life of modern Mexico as it has been since pre-Columbian times. A nutritious, unleavened bread, the corn tortilla is served at every meal and is the basis for many snacks. In Mexico, corn tortillas come in many colors, depending on the type of corn used to prepare them. Their size ranges from 2 inches to more than 18 inches in diameter according to how they'll be used—whole, cut or torn into different sizes or shapes, rolled, folded, stacked, grilled, fried, and, most importantly, filled.

NUTRITION FACTS PER TORTILLA

		Daily Values
Calories	69	3%
Total fat	1 g	1%
Saturated fat	0 g	0%
Cholesterol	0 mg	0%
Sodium	2 mg	0%
Carbohydrate	15 g	4%
Fiber	1 g	4%
Protein	2 g	

MAKE AHEAD

Prepare tortillas as directed. Stack them, alternating each tortilla with 2 layers of waxed paper. Place them in a freezer bag and freeze for up to 6 months. Before serving, thaw at room temperature.

Rick Strange / The Picture Cube

SALSAS

Avocados have been part of Mexican cuisine since the days of the Aztecs. Today they may be best known as the principal ingredient in guacamole. Most aficionados agree that keeping the guacamole slightly lumpy accentuates the avocado's buttery texture.

REGION: CENTRAL MEXICO

Guacamole

MAKES ABOUT 2½ CUPS   START TO FINISH: 20 MINUTES

MAKE AHEAD

Spoon guacamole into an airtight storage container. Cover surface with plastic wrap (to prevent browning) and chill for up to 12 hours.

2 medium ripe avocados (about 12 ounces total), halved, seeded, and peeled
1 tablespoon lemon juice
½ cup chopped, seeded tomato (1 small)
½ cup chopped onion (1 medium)
2 tablespoons snipped fresh cilantro
1 to 2 fresh serrano or jalapeño peppers, seeded and finely chopped
¼ teaspoon salt
   Chopped tomatoes (optional)
   Cilantro sprigs (optional)

1. Place avocado in a medium mixing bowl. Using a fork, mash the avocado along with the lemon juice (mixture will be lumpy).

2. Place chopped tomato, onion, cilantro, and serrano or jalapeño peppers in a food processor bowl or blender container. Cover and process or blend until finely chopped.

3. Stir tomato mixture and salt into mashed avocado until combined. Spoon mixture into a serving dish. If desired, garnish with additional chopped tomato and cilantro sprigs. Serve as a dip for chips or as a condiment for appetizers, soups, salads, or main dishes. Makes about 2½ cups.

ALL MEXICO

fresh Tomato Salsa
SALSA FRESCA

Salsa fresca is the fresh, homemade version of salsa—the condiment that has overtaken catsup in popularity in the United States. When prepared with vine-ripened tomatoes and other peak produce, it's easy to taste why this simple, uncooked sauce is in high demand.

MAKES ABOUT 3 CUPS   PREP: 20 MINUTES   CHILL: 1 HOUR

1½ cups finely chopped
    tomatoes (3 medium)
1 fresh Anaheim pepper,
    seeded and finely
    chopped, or one 4-ounce
    can diced green chili
    peppers, drained
¼ cup chopped green sweet
    pepper
¼ cup sliced green onions (2)
3 to 4 tablespoons snipped
    fresh cilantro or parsley
2 tablespoons lime juice or
    lemon juice
1 to 2 fresh jalapeño, serrano,
    fresno, or banana peppers,
    seeded and finely chopped
1 clove garlic, minced
⅛ teaspoon salt
⅛ teaspoon pepper

1. In a medium mixing bowl stir together chopped tomatoes, Anaheim pepper or canned chili peppers, sweet pepper, green onions, cilantro or parsley, lime juice or lemon juice, jalapeño pepper, garlic, salt, and pepper.*

2. Cover and chill at least 1 hour before serving. Serve as a dip for chips or as a condiment for appetizers or main dishes. Makes about 3 cups.

*Note: For a slightly smoother salsa, place 1 cup of the salsa in a food processor bowl or blender container. Cover and process or blend just until smooth. Stir into remaining salsa.

NO-FAT

NUTRITION FACTS
PER TABLESPOON

		Daily Values
Calories	2	0%
Total fat	0 g	0%
Saturated fat	0 g	0%
Cholesterol	0 mg	0%
Sodium	6 mg	0%
Carbohydrate	1 g	0%
Fiber	0 g	0%
Protein	0 g	

MAKE AHEAD

Spoon the salsa into a storage container. Cover and chill for up to 3 days.

24

Picante sauce is by definition hot and spicy. Its ingredients are similar to salsa fresca, except that the chilies are hotter and the sauce is cooked. The slow simmer allows the flavors to meld and tempers the heat. It can be used as a marinade, barbecue sauce, dip, or sauce for entrées.

REGION: CENTRAL MEXICO

Picante Sauce
SALSA PICANTE

MAKES ABOUT 2 CUPS   PREP: 15 MINUTES   COOK: 30 MINUTES   CHILL: 1 HOUR

NUTRITION FACTS
PER TABLESPOON

		Daily Values
Calories	6	0%
Total fat	0 g	0%
Saturated fat	0 g	0%
Cholesterol	0 mg	0%
Sodium	18 mg	0%
Carbohydrate	1 g	0%
Fiber	.3 g	1%
Protein	0 g	

MAKE AHEAD

Spoon the Picante Sauce into a storage container. Cover and chill for up to 1 week.

4 medium tomatoes (about 1¼ pounds total), seeded and cut up
1 medium onion, cut up
¼ cup snipped fresh cilantro or parsley
1 to 2 fresh jalapeño or serrano peppers, seeded and halved
2 cloves garlic, minced
½ cup finely chopped green sweet pepper (1 medium)
2 tablespoons lemon juice
1 tablespoon snipped fresh oregano or 1 teaspoon dried oregano, crushed
1 bay leaf
½ teaspoon sugar
¼ teaspoon salt

1. Place tomatoes in a blender container or food processor bowl. Cover and blend or process until coarsely chopped. Add onion, cilantro or parsley, jalapeño or serrano pepper, and garlic. Cover and blend or process until finely chopped.

2. Transfer tomato mixture to a medium saucepan. Stir in chopped sweet pepper, lemon juice, oregano, bay leaf, sugar, and salt. Bring to boiling. Reduce heat and simmer, uncovered, about 30 minutes or to desired consistency.

3. Remove bay leaf. Cool slightly. Cover and chill at least 1 hour before serving. Serve as a dip for chips, a barbecue sauce or marinade, or as a condiment for main dishes. Makes about 2 cups.

REGION: SOUTHERN MEXICO

Ranchero Salsa
SALSA RANCHERA

Broiling the tomatoes and chilies imparts a mellow, roasted flavor to this cooked sauce. The result is a chunky, ranch-style sauce that goes well over many foods.

MAKES ABOUT 1¼ CUPS   PREP: 30 MINUTES   COOK: 15 MINUTES

3 medium tomatoes (about 1 pound total), quartered
1 to 2 fresh jalapeño or serrano peppers, seeded and halved
½ cup chopped onion (1 medium)
1 clove garlic, minced
1 tablespoon olive oil or cooking oil
¼ teaspoon ground cumin

1. Place quartered tomatoes and jalapeño or serrano pepper halves, cut side down, on a broiler pan. Broil 4 inches from the heat for 9 to 11 minutes or until tomato skins and pepper skins start to blacken. Remove from broiler pan; cool.

2. Remove skin from tomatoes and peppers. Finely chop tomatoes and peppers.

3. In a small saucepan cook onion and garlic in hot oil for 3 minutes. Stir in chopped tomatoes, chopped peppers, and cumin. Bring to boiling. Reduce heat and simmer, uncovered, for 10 to 15 minutes or until most of the liquid has evaporated. Cool completely.

4. Serve with huevos rancheros, scrambled eggs, meatloaf, chicken, or fish. Makes about 1¼ cups.

NUTRITION FACTS PER TABLESPOON

		Daily Values
Calories	11	0%
Total fat	.6 g	0%
Saturated fat	.1 g	0%
Cholesterol	0 mg	0%
Sodium	2 mg	0%
Carbohydrate	1 g	0%
Fiber	.3 g	1%
Protein	0 g	

MAKE AHEAD

Spoon the salsa into a storage container. Cover and chill for up to 1 week.

Salsa verde is an uncooked salsa made with tomatillos. Although tomatillos look much like a small green tomato with husks and may be called Mexican green tomatoes, botanically they're not related. The sauce is popular in central Mexico where it's blended on a molcajete, *a three-legged basalt version of the mortar, with a* tejolote *(pestle). Our quick version requires only chopping.*

REGION: CENTRAL MEXICO

Salsa Verde

MAKES ABOUT 2 CUPS   PREP: 30 MINUTES   CHILL: 4 HOURS

NUTRITION FACTS
PER TABLESPOON

		Daily Values
Calories	3	0%
Total fat	0 g	0%
Saturated fat	0 g	0%
Cholesterol	0 mg	0%
Sodium	17 mg	0%
Carbohydrate	1 g	0%
Fiber	0 g	0%
Protein	0 g	

6 to 8 tomatillos or one 13-ounce can tomatillos, rinsed and drained
¼ cup snipped fresh cilantro or parsley
2 tablespoons finely chopped red onion
1 fresh serrano or jalapeño pepper, seeded and finely chopped
¼ teaspoon salt
¼ teaspoon sugar

1. Remove husks from fresh tomatillos; rinse. Finely chop the fresh or canned tomatillos (you should have about 2 cups).

2. In a small mixing bowl stir together chopped tomatillos, cilantro or parsley, onion, serrano or jalapeño pepper, salt, and sugar. Cover and chill at least 4 hours before serving, stirring occasionally.

3. Serve as a dip for chips or as a condiment for tacos, tostadas, or grilled meats and fish. Makes about 2 cups.

MAKE AHEAD

Spoon the salsa into a storage container. Cover and chill for up to 3 days.

REGION: CENTRAL MEXICO

*C*hipotle Chili Salsa
SALSA DE CHILE CHIPOTLE

This relishlike salsa has a hot, smoky flavor that comes from the chipotle pepper. Chipotles are jalapeños that have been smoked and dried—a process that is as old as the Aztecs.

MAKES ABOUT 1½ CUPS   PREP: 55 MINUTES   STAND: 30 MINUTES

3 **dried chipotle peppers or 3 canned chipotle peppers in adobo sauce, rinsed, drained, seeded, and finely chopped**
6 to 8 **tomatillos or one 13-ounce can tomatillos, rinsed and drained**
¼ **cup chopped onion**
1 **tablespoon snipped fresh thyme or ½ teaspoon dried thyme, crushed**
2 **cloves garlic, minced**
1 **teaspoon brown sugar**
¼ **teaspoon salt**

1. Cut dried peppers open; discard stems and seeds. Chop peppers into tiny pieces. Place in a small bowl and cover with *boiling water*. Let stand 45 to 60 minutes to soften; drain well.

2. Meanwhile, remove husks from fresh tomatillos; rinse. Finely chop the fresh or canned tomatillos (you should have about 2 cups). In a medium mixing bowl combine pepper pieces, chopped tomatillos, onion, thyme, garlic, brown sugar, and salt.

3. Cover and let stand at room temperature for 30 minutes to blend flavors. Serve as a dip for chips or as a condiment for grilled meats, hot dogs, burgers, steaks, or poultry. Makes about 1½ cups.

NUTRITION FACTS PER TABLESPOON

		Daily Values
Calories	8	0%
Total fat	.1 g	0%
Saturated fat	0 g	0%
Cholesterol	0 mg	0%
Sodium	36 mg	1%
Carbohydrate	2 g	0%
Fiber	.3 g	1%
Protein	0 g	

MAKE AHEAD

Spoon the salsa into a storage container. Cover and chill for up to 1 week.

NEW MEXICO

*Chili Colorado, the basic
red chili sauce of New
Mexico, is an all-purpose
sauce used on everything
from huevos rancheros,
enchiladas, and tamales to
grilled meats and poultry.
There are many versions
of this classic sauce,
including those made with
powdered chilies and with
or without tomatoes. The
flavor should be both
sharp and smooth.*

Chili Colorado
CHILE COLORADO

MAKES ABOUT 2 CUPS   PREP: 1 HOUR   COOK: 20 MINUTES

NUTRITION FACTS
PER TABLESPOON

		Daily Values
Calories	17	0%
Total fat	.4 g	0%
Saturated fat	.1 g	0%
Cholesterol	0 mg	0%
Sodium	59 mg	2%
Carbohydrate	3 g	0%
Fiber	2 g	6%
Protein	0 g	

MAKE AHEAD

Spoon sauce into
an airtight storage
container. Cover and
chill for up to 1 week.

12 **dried ancho peppers or dried
mild New Mexico red
peppers (4 ounces)**
4 **dried chipotle peppers or
4 canned chipotle peppers
in adobo sauce, rinsed,
drained, seeded, and
finely chopped**
3 **cups water**
½ **cup chopped onion
(1 medium)**
1 **tablespoon snipped fresh
oregano or 1 teaspoon
dried oregano, crushed**
3 **cloves garlic, minced**
1 **tablespoon olive oil or
cooking oil**
1½ **cups chopped tomato
(2 medium)**
¼ **teaspoon salt**
¼ **teaspoon ground cumin**

1. Cut dried ancho or dried New Mexico red
peppers and, if using, dried chipotle peppers. Open
peppers; discard stems and seeds. Cut peppers into
small pieces. Bring water to boiling; remove from
heat. Add peppers and let stand for 45 to 60 minutes
to soften. Do not drain.

2. Meanwhile, in a large skillet cook onion, oregano,
and garlic in hot oil for 3 minutes. Remove from
heat; set aside.

3. Place half of the undrained dried peppers (and
canned chipotle peppers, if using) and *half* of the
chopped tomatoes in a food processor bowl or
blender container. Cover and process or blend until
nearly smooth. Strain through a fine sieve to remove
pepper skins and tomato skins and seeds; discard
skins and seeds. Repeat blending and straining with
remaining peppers and tomatoes. Add strained
mixture to onion mixture in skillet along with salt
and cumin.

4. Bring to boiling. Reduce heat and simmer,
uncovered, for 20 to 25 minutes or to desired
consistency. Serve with huevos rancheros,
enchiladas, tamales, or grilled meats and poultry.
Makes about 2 cups.

TEXAS & MEXICO

Mango Salsa
SALSA DE MANGO

Long popular in Mexico, mangoes now are readily available in U.S. supermarkets. A colorful addition to salsas, their peachlike flavor and juiciness provide an interesting contrast to the lime juice.

MAKES ABOUT 2 CUPS   PREP: 20 MINUTES   CHILL: 2 HOURS

1½ **cups chopped, peeled mango, papaya, peaches, plums, and/or pineapple**
½ **cup chopped red or green sweet pepper**
¼ **cup thinly sliced green onions (2)**
¼ **cup snipped fresh cilantro or parsley**
2 **tablespoons lime juice or lemon juice**
1 **to 2 fresh jalapeño or serrano peppers, seeded and finely chopped, or 2 tablespoons finely chopped fresh Anaheim pepper**

1. In a medium mixing bowl stir together fruit, sweet pepper, green onions, cilantro or parsley, lime juice or lemon juice, and jalapeño, serrano, or Anaheim pepper. Cover; chill at least 2 hours before serving.

2. Serve as a dip for chips or fresh vegetables or as a condiment for tacos, quesadillas, burgers, steaks, chicken, or fish. Makes about 2 cups.

NO-FAT

NUTRITION FACTS
PER TABLESPOON

		Daily Values
Calories	5	0%
Total fat	0 g	0%
Saturated fat	0 g	0%
Cholesterol	0 mg	0%
Sodium	0 mg	0%
Carbohydrate	1 g	0%
Fiber	0 g	0%
Protein	0 g	

MAKE AHEAD

Spoon the salsa into a storage container. Cover and chill for up to 2 days.

MANGOES

Depending on the variety of mango, the color will vary when ripe from red to yellow to green. Mangoes should be fully colored, have a fruity aroma, and give slightly when pressed. To remove the stubborn seed, place the mango upright and cut through the mango, sliding the knife close to the long, flat seed. Repeat on the other side of the seed. To slice the 2 halves into cubes, cut crosshatches through the flesh, just to the peel. Bend the peel back and carefully slide the knife between the peel and flesh to separate. A curved grapefruit knife works well for this task.

SALADS AND VEGETABLES

ALL MEXICO

*C*hayote Salad
ENSALADA DE CHAYOTE

MAKES 6 SIDE-DISH SERVINGS   PREP: 30 MINUTES   MARINATE: 3 TO 24 HOURS

3 medium chayotes, peeled, seeded, and cut into ½-inch pieces
1 cup canned garbanzo beans, rinsed and drained

MARINADE
¼ cup lemon juice
¼ cup olive oil or salad oil
¼ cup water
1 tablespoon snipped fresh basil or 1 teaspoon dried basil, crushed
½ teaspoon sugar
¼ teaspoon salt
2 cloves garlic, minced

¼ cup sliced pitted ripe olives
6 lettuce leaves
2 tablespoons chopped red onion
2 medium tomatoes, cut into wedges

1. In a medium saucepan cook chayotes, covered, in a small amount of *boiling salted water* for 5 to 6 minutes or until tender; drain. Rinse with cold water to stop cooking; drain well. Transfer to a medium mixing bowl; add garbanzo beans.

2. For marinade, in a screw-top jar combine lemon juice, olive oil or salad oil, water, basil, sugar, salt, and garlic. Cover and shake well. Pour marinade over chayote mixture, stirring to coat well. Cover and marinate in the refrigerator for 3 to 24 hours, stirring occasionally.

3. To serve, drain chayote mixture, reserving marinade. Stir in olives. Spoon chayote mixture onto 6 lettuce-lined plates. Top each serving with chopped red onion and tomato wedges. Drizzle with some of the reserved marinade. Makes 6 side-dish servings.

Long a favorite in the Americas, chayote (chaw-YOTE-ee), or mirliton as it's called in the southern United States, is a pear-shaped vegetable that requires cooking. The word chayote is virtually unchanged from the Aztec word chayotli. *With a crisp, firm texture and a moist flesh, a chayote tastes like a cross between a cucumber and an apple. The mild flavor works well with more assertive flavors such as this tangy vinaigrette dressing. Look for small, firm, unblemished chayotes ranging in color from cream to pale green and deep green. They may be stored in a plastic bag for up to 2 weeks in the refrigerator.*

LOW-FAT

NUTRITION FACTS PER SERVING

		Daily Values
Calories	83	4%
Total fat	5 g	7%
Saturated fat	1 g	2%
Cholesterol	0 g	0%
Sodium	175 mg	7%
Carbohydrate	10 g	3%
Fiber	3 g	12%
Protein	2 g	

REGION: CENTRAL MEXICO

This play on the words "pico de gallo," or rooster's beak, refers to a way of eating the salad, not its content. People used to eat it by picking up the pieces with their fingertips, mimicking the way a rooster pecks corn. Share the amusing story with guests when you serve this wonderful combination of flavors and textures—even if you choose to eat it with a fork.

Jicama Pico de Gallo Salad
ENSALADA DE JÍCAMA

MAKES 6 SIDE-DISH SERVINGS   START TO FINISH: 30 MINUTES

SALAD
  6 **lettuce leaves**
  ½ **of a medium red onion, thinly sliced**
  2 **cups peeled jicama cut into thin bite-size strips**
  1 **large red, green, or yellow sweet pepper, cut into thin bite-size strips**
  1 **cup carrot cut into thin bite-size strips**

DRESSING
  1 **teaspoon finely shredded orange peel**
  ½ **cup orange juice**
  3 **tablespoons olive oil or salad oil**
  1 **tablespoon snipped fresh cilantro or parsley**
  ¼ **teaspoon ground cumin**
    Dash salt
    Dash ground black pepper

1. Arrange lettuce leaves on 6 salad plates. Arrange red onion slices on top of lettuce. Divide jicama, sweet pepper, and carrot strips among each plate.

2. For dressing, in a screw-top jar combine the orange peel, orange juice, olive oil or salad oil, cilantro or parsley, cumin, salt, and black pepper. Cover and shake well. Drizzle dressing over salads. Makes 6 side-dish servings.

NUTRITION FACTS PER SERVING

		Daily Values
Calories	113	5%
Total fat	7 g	10%
Saturated fat	1 g	4%
Cholesterol	0 mg	0%
Sodium	34 mg	1%
Carbohydrate	12 g	3%
Fiber	1 g	5%
Protein	1 g	

MAKE AHEAD

Prepare the dressing as directed. Cover and chill for up to 2 days. Cut up onion, jicama, sweet pepper, and carrot. Place in separate storage containers and chill for up to 24 hours. Assemble as directed.

JICAMA

Jicama (HE-kuh-muh) is a large, tuberous root vegetable with pale brown, thin skin. Raw jicama will have a clean crisp bite and a mildly sweet flavor. Peel before using whether cooked or raw. Look for firm, heavy jicamas with unblemished skin. The larger jicamas may be more fibrous and better suited to cooking. They are available year-round in large supermarkets and Mexican specialty stores.

ALL MEXICO

Christmas Eve Salad

ENSALADA DE NOCHEBUENA

This tasty melange of fresh fruit is accented with colorful beets and crisp jicama strips. Garnished with nuts and pomegranate seeds, it is traditionally served with turkey—another food native to Mexico—after the midnight mass on Christmas Eve.

MAKES 6 SIDE-DISH SERVINGS   PREP: 30 MINUTES   CHILL: 2 TO 24 HOURS

DRESSING
- ⅓ cup olive oil
- 3 tablespoons vinegar
- 2 tablespoons lime juice
- 2 tablespoons sugar

SALAD
- 2 medium oranges
- 2 cups fresh cubed pineapple or one 20-ounce can juice-packed pineapple chunks, drained
- 1 large apple, cored and sliced
  Romaine leaves
- 4 cups shredded leaf lettuce
- 1 medium banana, sliced
- 1 16-ounce can sliced beets, rinsed and drained
- 1 cup jicama cut into thin bite-size strips
- ½ cup pine nuts or peanuts
- ½ cup pomegranate seeds or finely chopped red onion

1. For dressing, in a screw-top jar combine olive oil, vinegar, lime juice, and sugar. Cover and shake well. Chill for 2 to 24 hours.

2. Peel and section the oranges over a large mixing bowl to catch the juice. Add orange sections, pineapple, and apple slices to the bowl. Toss to coat all of the fruit with orange juice. Cover and chill for 2 to 24 hours.

3. To serve, line 6 salad plates with romaine leaves. Top with shredded lettuce. Add banana slices to the fruit mixture; toss to coat bananas with juice. Drain the fruit mixture. Divide the fruit mixture, beets, and jicama among the salad plates. Sprinkle each serving with pine nuts or peanuts and pomegranate seeds or red onion. Shake the salad dressing and pour some over each salad. Makes 6 side-dish servings.

NUTRITION FACTS PER SERVING		
		Daily Values
Calories	303	15%
Total fat	19 g	29%
Saturated fat	3 g	13%
Cholesterol	0 mg	0%
Sodium	176 mg	7%
Carbohydrate	34 g	11%
Fiber	4 g	15%
Protein	6 g	

Chilies stuffed with cheese are a popular dish. Some restaurants in New Mexico take it one step further by stuffing the chilies with mashed potatoes. In this case, colorful sweet potatoes complement the cheese and peppers.

NEW MEXICO

Potato- and Cheese-Stuffed Chili Peppers

CHILES RELLENOS DE PAPA Y QUESO

MAKES 6 SIDE-DISH SERVINGS   PREP: 30 MINUTES   BAKE: 25 MINUTES

LOW-FAT

NUTRITION FACTS PER SERVING

		Daily Values
Calories	79	3%
Total fat	2 g	3%
Saturated fat	1 g	6%
Cholesterol	9 mg	2%
Sodium	118 mg	4%
Carbohydrate	11 g	3%
Fiber	2 g	8%
Protein	4 g	

M AKE   A HEAD

Prepare and stuff the peppers. Cover and chill for up to 24 hours. Bake as directed, allowing a few extra minutes to heat through.

3 large fresh Anaheim or
   poblano peppers or
3 small sweet peppers

FILLING
1½ cups chopped sweet potatoes
   or potatoes
1 to 3 tablespoons milk
⅓ cup finely chopped green
   onions (3)
2 teaspoons chili powder
1 clove garlic, minced
½ cup shredded asadero, queso
   quesadilla, Chihuahua, or
   Monterey Jack cheese
1 beaten egg white

Nonstick spray coating

1. Cut the peppers in half lengthwise. Remove seeds and membranes. In a saucepan cook peppers in *boiling water* about 5 minutes or until crisp-tender. Drain well.

2. Meanwhile, cook potatoes, covered, in *boiling lightly salted water* for 15 to 20 minutes or until tender; drain. Mash potatoes, adding milk, *1 tablespoon* at a time, until potato mixture is fluffy. Stir in green onions, chili powder, and garlic. Stir in ¼ *cup* of the shredded cheese and the egg white.

3. Spoon potato mixture into peppers. Spray a 3-quart rectangular baking dish with cooking spray. Place stuffed peppers close together in baking dish.

4. Bake, covered, in a 350° oven 25 to 30 minutes or until heated through. Sprinkle tops with remaining shredded cheese. Makes 6 side-dish servings.

This spicy side dish celebrates many of the foods that existed in Mexico before the Spaniards arrived. Chayotes, chilies, sweet peppers, tomatoes, corn— even a type of oregano— were among the bounty found in the Americas. Stuffed chayotes are a common dish in Mexico.

TEXAS & MEXICO

Corn- and Pepper-Stuffed Chayote
CHAYOTES RELLENOS DE ELOTE Y CHILE POBLANO

MAKES 6 SIDE-DISH SERVINGS   PREP: 55 MINUTES   BAKE: 30 MINUTES

LOW-FAT

NUTRITION FACTS PER SERVING

		Daily Values
Calories	94	4%
Total fat	3 g	4%
Saturated fat	.3 g	1%
Cholesterol	0 mg	0%
Sodium	125 mg	5%
Carbohydrate	17 mg	5%
Fiber	2 g	9%
Protein	3 g	

MAKE AHEAD

Prepare and stuff the chayote. Cover and chill for up to 24 hours. Bake as directed, allowing a few extra minutes to heat through.

1 dried chipotle pepper or
   2 dried ancho peppers
3 medium chayotes or large
   zucchini (1½ pounds total)

FILLING
1 medium yellow or green
   sweet pepper, chopped
½ cup chopped onion
1 tablespoon olive oil or
   cooking oil
1½ cups frozen whole kernel
   corn
¾ cup chopped tomato
   (1 medium)
2 teaspoons snipped fresh
   oregano or ½ teaspoon
   dried oregano, crushed
½ cup soft bread crumbs
¼ teaspoon salt
⅛ teaspoon ground black
   pepper

Nonstick spray coating

1. Cut the chipotle or ancho peppers open; discard stems and seeds. Cut peppers into extra-small pieces. Place in a small bowl and cover with *boiling water.* Let stand 45 to 60 minutes to soften. Drain well.

2. Meanwhile, halve the chayotes or zucchini lengthwise; remove seeds. Scoop out the pulp of the chayotes or zucchini, leaving a ¼-inch-thick shell. Chop pulp and set aside.

3. Cook chayote shells in *boiling lightly salted water* for 5 minutes. Invert the shells and drain. (Do not precook zucchini shells.)

4. For filling, in a large skillet cook the sweet pepper and onion in hot oil for 3 minutes. Stir in chopped chayote or zucchini pulp, drained pepper pieces, corn, tomato, and oregano. Cook, uncovered, for 5 minutes, stirring frequently. Remove from heat. Stir in bread crumbs, salt, and black pepper.

5. Spray a 2-quart rectangular baking dish with cooking spray. Arrange chayote or zucchini shells, cut sides up, in prepared dish. Spoon filling into shells. Bake, covered, in a 350° oven for about 30 minutes or until heated through. Makes 6 side-dish servings.

REGION: CENTRAL MEXICO

Avocado Soup
CREMA DE AGUACATE

The idea for the soup course, both the hot and chilled versions, probably was brought to Mexico from Spain. The readily available avocado would have been a natural ingredient to mash and blend with a broth, creating a soup with a creamy consistency.

MAKES 3 CUPS (6 SIDE-DISH SERVINGS)   PREP: 20 MINUTES   CHILL: 1 TO 24 HOURS

2 **medium ripe avocados, halved, seeded, peeled, and cut up**
⅓ **cup chopped onion (1 small)**
¼ **cup shredded carrot**
1 **clove garlic, minced**
2½ **cups reduced-sodium chicken broth**
½ **cup light dairy sour cream**
 Few dashes bottled hot pepper sauce
 Cilantro sprigs (optional)
 Chopped tomato (optional)

1. In a blender container or food processor bowl combine avocados, onion, carrot, garlic, and *1 cup* of the chicken broth. Cover and blend or process until almost smooth.

2. Add remaining chicken broth, sour cream, and bottled hot pepper sauce. Cover and blend or process until smooth. Pour soup into a bowl. Cover surface with plastic wrap and chill for 1 to 24 hours.*

3. To serve, ladle soup into chilled soup cups. Garnish with cilantro and chopped tomato, if desired. Makes 3 cups (6 side-dish servings).

***Note:** If you like your soup hot, warm the soup in a saucepan for 10 minutes over medium heat, but do not boil.

NUTRITION FACTS PER SERVING		
		Daily Values
Calories	155	7%
Total fat	11 g	16%
Saturated fat	2 g	12%
Cholesterol	3 mg	0%
Sodium	297 mg	12%
Carbohydrate	13 g	4%
Fiber	3 g	12%
Protein	4 g	

Rick Strange / The Picture Cube

MEATS

REGION: NORTHERN MEXICO

Fajitas

MAKES 4 SERVINGS   PREP: 1 HOUR   MARINATE: 2 TO 4 HOURS   COOK: 6 MINUTES

12 ounces boneless beef skirt
    steak or flank steak

MARINADE
⅓ cup cooking oil
⅓ cup lime juice
2 fresh jalapeño peppers,
    seeded and chopped
3 tablespoons sliced green
    onions (2)
2 tablespoons snipped fresh
    cilantro
¼ teaspoon salt
2 cloves garlic, minced

8 8-inch flour tortillas
1 tablespoon cooking oil
1 medium onion, thinly sliced
    and separated into rings
1 medium red or green sweet
    pepper, cut into thin strips
¾ cup chopped tomato
    (1 medium)
    Guacamole (see recipe,
    page 22) (optional)
    Salsa (optional)
    Dairy sour cream (optional)

1. Trim fat from meat. Partially freeze meat for about 30 minutes. Thinly slice across the grain into bite-size strips. Place strips in a plastic bag set in a deep bowl.

2. Meanwhile, for marinade, in a small mixing bowl combine the ⅓ cup cooking oil, lime juice, jalapeño peppers, green onions, cilantro, salt, and garlic. Pour marinade over beef strips in bag. Close bag tightly; turn to coat beef strips. Marinate in the refrigerator for 2 to 4 hours, turning bag occasionally.

3. Wrap tortillas tightly in foil. Heat in a 350° oven about 10 minutes or until heated through.

4. Meanwhile, drain beef strips; discard marinade. In a large skillet heat the 1 tablespoon cooking oil over medium-high heat. Add onion rings and sweet pepper strips. Cook and stir about 3 minutes or until crisp-tender. Remove vegetables from skillet.

5. Add beef to the hot skillet. Cook and stir for 2 to 3 minutes or until done. Drain well. Return all vegetables to skillet. Stir in chopped tomato. Cook and stir for 1 to 2 minutes or until heated through.

6. To serve, fill warm tortillas with beef-vegetable mixture. If desired, top with Guacamole, salsa, and sour cream. Roll up tortillas. Makes 4 servings.

Delivered sizzling from kitchen to customer, fajitas are hot in North American restaurants. The word "fajita" comes from the Spanish faja, for the band of meat from the short plate—skirt steak in English. Traditionally, cowboys along the northern Mexican border barbecued the cut, known as arrachera, over their campfires. In the 1970s clever restaurateurs took it a step further by marinating this less tender cut of beef, grilling it with vegetables, and serving it with a flourish. The once obscure and inexpensive cut of beef is now hard to find and pricey, but flank steak is a good substitute.

NUTRITION FACTS PER SERVING

		Daily Values
Calories	479	23%
Total fat	19 g	28%
Saturated fat	4 g	21%
Cholesterol	40 mg	13%
Sodium	801 mg	33%
Carbohydrate	54 g	18%
Fiber	1 g	4%
Protein	23 g	

REGION: SONORA

Chimichangas

MAKES 8 CHIMICHANGAS   PREP: 30 MINUTES   FRY: 2 MINUTES PER BATCH

Several Mexican food authorities tell us chivichangas *would be more accurate, but* chimichangas *is the term most of us recognize for crispy, stuffed tortillas. Large flour tortillas are filled with a variety of meat or fruit fillings, rolled into an envelope shape, and usually deep-fat fried. To cut 100 calories and 12 grams total fat, use our simple method for Baked Chimichangas.*

NUTRITION FACTS
PER CHIMICHANGA

		Daily Values
Calories	372	18%
Total fat	27 g	40%
Saturated fat	8 g	38%
Cholesterol	51 mg	16%
Sodium	315 mg	13%
Carbohydrate	17 g	5%
Fiber	1 g	5%
Protein	16 g	

MAKE AHEAD

Prepare Spicy Beef Filling as directed. Cover and chill for up to 2 days or freeze for up to 6 months. Thaw overnight in refrigerator before using.

1 recipe Spicy Beef Filling
8 10-inch flour tortillas
1 cup shredded cheddar cheese or Monterey Jack cheese
Cooking oil
4 cups shredded lettuce
Salsa (optional)
Guacamole (see recipe, page 22) (optional)

1. Prepare Spicy Beef Filling; set aside.

2. Wrap tortillas tightly in foil. Heat in a 350° oven about 10 minutes or until heated through.

3. Spoon about ⅓ cup of the filling down center of each tortilla. Top each with about 2 *tablespoons* of the cheese. Fold opposite sides of tortilla in over the filling. Fold up the tortilla, starting from the bottom. Secure ends with wooden toothpicks.

4. In a deep saucepan heat about 1 inch cooking oil to 375°. Fry filled tortillas, 2 or 3 at a time, about 1 minute on each side or until crisp and golden brown. Drain on paper towels. Keep chimichangas warm in a 300° oven while frying remaining ones.

5. Remove toothpicks. Place chimichangas on top of the shredded lettuce. If desired, top with salsa and Guacamole. Makes 8 chimichangas.

SPICY BEEF FILLING

In a large skillet cook 1 pound *lean ground beef*, ½ cup chopped *onion*, and 2 cloves *garlic*, minced, until meat is brown and onion is tender. Drain off fat. Stir in one 4½-ounce can *diced green chili peppers*, drained; 1 tablespoon *chili powder*; ¼ teaspoon *ground cumin*; ⅛ teaspoon *salt*; and ⅛ teaspoon *ground black pepper*; heat through. Makes 3 cups.

BAKED CHIMICHANGAS

Prepare as above through Step 3. Place chimichangas on a large baking sheet and brush with 1 tablespoon *cooking oil*. Bake in a 350° oven for 30 to 40 minutes or until golden brown and heated through. Serve as directed above.

ALL MEXICO

Meatball Soup
ALBÓNDIGAS

MAKES ABOUT 8 CUPS (6 SERVINGS)   PREP: 30 MINUTES   COOK: 30 MINUTES

MEATBALLS
- 1 **slightly beaten egg or egg white**
- 3 **tablespoons long-grain rice**
- 2 **teaspoons snipped fresh oregano or 1 teaspoon dried oregano, crushed**
- ¼ **teaspoon salt**
- ⅛ **teaspoon ground black pepper**
- 1 **pound lean ground beef or ground pork**

SOUP
- 2 **14½-ounce cans beef broth**
- 1 **cup water**
- ⅓ **cup tomato paste**
- 2 **cups cubed potatoes (2 medium)**
- 1 **cup thinly sliced carrots (2 medium)**
- 1 **medium onion, thinly sliced**
- ½ **cup frozen peas**

1. For meatballs, in a medium mixing bowl combine the egg, uncooked rice, oregano, salt, and black pepper. Stir in meat; mix well. Shape meat mixture into 1-inch meatballs.

2. For soup, in a large saucepan combine beef broth, water, and tomato paste. Bring to boiling. Add meatballs and simmer, covered, for 15 to 20 minutes or until meat is no longer pink inside and rice is tender.

3. Add potatoes, carrots, and onion to saucepan. Cook, covered, about 15 minutes more or until vegetables are crisp-tender. Stir in peas and heat through. Makes about 8 cups (6 servings).

Albóndigas, or meatballs, often are used in soup in Mexico, especially in the beef-producing North. The meatballs usually are combined with rice and poached in beef broth with commonly found vegetables. Use the leanest ground meat to avoid extra fat. This soup isn't highly spiced, but salsa or chopped chilies could be served on the side for those who want more fire.

LOW-FAT

NUTRITION FACTS PER SERVING

		Daily Values
Calories	259	12%
Total fat	9 g	13%
Saturated fat	3 g	16%
Cholesterol	83 mg	27%
Sodium	627 mg	26%
Carbohydrate	26 g	8%
Fiber	3 g	13%
Protein	19 g	

MAKE AHEAD

Mix and shape the meatballs. Arrange on a baking sheet lined with waxed paper. Freeze until firm. Place meatballs in a freezer container or bag and freeze for up to 6 months. Thaw before adding to soup.

A savory country stew, mole de olla takes its name from mole, *a mixture simmered in a decorated earthenware pot, or* olla. *The stew is a harmonious combination of New World vegetables—mild ancho peppers, squash, potatoes, tomatoes, corn— and Old World beef.*

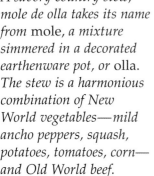

ALL MEXICO

Beef Stew in a Pot
MOLE DE OLLA

MAKES ABOUT 8 CUPS (4 SERVINGS)   PREP: 20 MINUTES   COOK: 1⅔ HOURS

NUTRITION FACTS PER SERVING		
		Daily Values
Calories	336	16%
Total fat	14 g	20%
Saturated fat	4 g	21%
Cholesterol	63 mg	21%
Sodium	340 mg	14%
Carbohydrate	33 g	11%
Fiber	5 g	18%
Protein	23 g	

MAKE AHEAD

Prepare stew through Step 3. Cool slightly. Cover and chill for up to 24 hours. To serve, bring stew to boiling. Continue with Step 4.

12 ounces beef stew meat,* cut into ¾-inch cubes
1 tablespoon cooking oil
2 cups water
½ teaspoon salt
¼ teaspoon ground black pepper
1 to 2 dried ancho peppers
2 cups chopped, peeled tomatoes (2 large) or one 14½-ounce can tomatoes, cut up
1 medium onion, cut up
¼ teaspoon ground cumin
2 cloves garlic, minced
2 medium potatoes, cut into 1-inch cubes
1 large fresh ear of corn, cut into 1-inch pieces, or 1 cup frozen whole kernel corn
1 medium zucchini or yellow summer squash, halved lengthwise and sliced 1 inch thick

1. In a large saucepan brown meat in hot oil. Drain off fat. Add water, salt, and black pepper to saucepan. Bring to boiling. Reduce heat and simmer, covered, for 1 hour.

2. Meanwhile, cut dried peppers open; discard stems and seeds. Cut peppers into small pieces. Place in a small bowl and cover with *boiling water*. Let stand 45 to 60 minutes to soften. Drain well.

3. In a blender container or food processor bowl, combine drained pepper pieces, tomatoes or undrained canned tomatoes, onion, cumin, and garlic. Cover and blend or process until nearly smooth. Stir into saucepan mixture.

4. Add potatoes and corn. Bring to boiling. Reduce heat and simmer, covered, for 30 minutes.

5. Stir in zucchini or summer squash. Cook about 10 minutes more or until meat and vegetables are tender. Makes about 8 cups (4 servings).

*Note: Beef round steak or chuck roast are good cuts to use for stew meat. Remove and discard any excess fat from the meat before cutting it into cubes.

There's no denying that preparing tamales is a labor of love. The packets of steamed masa dough filled with savory pork and Chili Colorado or other regional favorites are always found on the fiesta table in Mexico. Invite guests to spread the tamal *dough on corn husks, aluminum foil, or cooking parchment. The aroma, texture, and flavor of fresh tamales won't soon be forgotten. (See the cover photograph.)*

NUTRITION FACTS PER TAMALE

		Daily Values
Calories	198	9%
Total fat	12 g	18%
Saturated fat	3 g	16%
Cholesterol	19 mg	6%
Sodium	199 mg	8%
Carbohydrate	15 g	5%
Fiber	3 g	13%
Protein	6 g	

MAKE AHEAD

Wrap and freeze the cooked tamales in the corn husks. To serve, thaw overnight in the refrigerator. Place the tamales in a steamer basket over gently boiling water for 15 to 20 minutes or until heated through.

REGIONS: CENTRAL & WEST-CENTRAL MEXICO

Shredded Pork Tamales

TAMALES DE CERDO DESHEBRADO

MAKES ABOUT 16 TAMALES   SOAK: 4 TO 24 HOURS   PREP: 1 HOUR   COOK: 40 MINUTES

16 dried corn husks (about 8 inches long and 6 inches wide at the top)

2 cups masa harina tortilla flour

1 cup warm water

⅔ cup shortening

½ teaspoon salt

1½ cups Shredded Savory Pork (see recipe, page 45)

⅔ cup Chili Colorado (see recipe, page 28)

1. Soak the corn husks in *warm water* for 4 to 24 hours to soften. Pat with paper towels to remove excess moisture.

2. For tamale dough, in a large mixing bowl stir together tortilla flour and water. Cover and let stand for 20 minutes (mixture will appear dry). Beat shortening and salt with an electric mixer on medium speed for 1 minute. Gradually beat in flour mixture until combined (mixture should resemble a thick, creamy paste).

3. Meanwhile, for filling, in a medium saucepan combine Shredded Savory Pork and Chili Colorado; heat through.

4. To assemble each tamale, spread about 2 tablespoons of the dough into a 5×4-inch rectangle on each corn husk, spreading a long side of the dough to the long edge of the wrapper. (If husks are small, overlap two small ones to form one.) Spoon about 1 tablespoon of the filling lengthwise down the center of the dough. Fold the long edge of wrapper over the filling so dough edges meet. Continue rolling up wrapper. Tie ends securely with pieces of corn husk or string.

5. Place a mound of extra corn husks (or a foil ball) in the center of a steamer basket. Lean tamales in basket. Bring water to boiling in a large saucepan; reduce heat. Place steamer basket over boiling water. Cover and steam for 40 to 45 minutes or until tamales pull away from corn husks, adding more water to saucepan as necessary. Makes about 16 tamales.

REGION: PUEBLA

Shredded Savory Pork
TINGA POBLANA

MAKES 8 SERVINGS (ABOUT 3 CUPS COOKED MEAT)   PREP: 15 MINUTES   COOK: 2½ HOURS

1 2-pound boneless pork blade roast
  Water
2 large onions, quartered
3 fresh jalapeño peppers, cut up
8 cloves garlic, minced
2 teaspoons ground coriander
2 teaspoons ground cumin
2 teaspoons dried oregano, crushed
½ teaspoon salt
½ teaspoon ground black pepper

1. Trim fat from meat. Place roast in a large saucepan or pot; add enough water to nearly cover. Stir in onions, cut-up jalapeño peppers, garlic, ground coriander, cumin, oregano, salt, and black pepper. Bring to boiling. Reduce heat and simmer, covered, for 2½ to 3 hours or until very tender.

2. Remove meat from liquid with a slotted spoon; discard cooking liquid. When cool enough to handle, shred the meat, pulling through it with 2 forks in opposite directions. Use as a filling for tamales or tacos. Makes 8 servings (about 3 cups cooked meat).

CROCKERY-COOKER DIRECTIONS

Trim fat from meat. If necessary, cut meat to fit in a 3½- or 4-quart crockery cooker. Add *1 cup* water and the remaining ingredients. Cover and cook on low-heat setting for 8 to 10 hours or on high-heat setting for 4 to 5 hours. Continue with Step 2 as directed.

Pork is the most frequently used meat in Mexico. This nicely seasoned pork filling is used to prepare Shredded Pork Tamales (see page 44) and is a change of pace for tacos. The ground coriander in the recipe tastes like a blend of lemon and sage. Don't confuse it with the leaves of the coriander plant, also known as cilantro. The flavor of the latter is different, and the two are not interchangeable.

NUTRITION FACTS PER SERVING

		Daily Values
Calories	188	9%
Total fat	12 g	17%
Saturated fat	4 g	19%
Cholesterol	74 mg	24%
Sodium	192 mg	8%
Carbohydrate	0 g	0%
Fiber	0 g	0%
Protein	20 g	

MAKE AHEAD

Place shredded meat in a freezer container. Cover and freeze for up to 6 months. Thaw overnight in refrigerator before using.

REGION: PUEBLA

Stuffed Chilies in Walnut Sauce

CHILES EN NOGADA

MAKES 6 SERVINGS   PREP: 30 MINUTES   BAKE: 20 MINUTES

Reminiscent of the colors of the Mexican flag— green, white, and red— this classic dish of stuffed green chilies and white walnut sauce often is garnished with red pomegranate seeds and served on Mexican Independence Day, September 15. For the striking presentation shown in the photograph on page 47, spoon a ring of Chili Colorado around the edge of a dinner plate, fill the center with some of the Walnut Sauce, and place the filled pepper in the middle of the plate.

NUTRITION FACTS PER SERVING

		Daily Values
Calories	340	16%
Total fat	20 g	30%
Saturated fat	4 g	20%
Cholesterol	52 mg	17%
Sodium	546 mg	22%
Carbohydrate	29 g	9%
Fiber	5 g	20%
Protein	16 g	

MAKE AHEAD

Cover and chill the filled peppers and the sauce for up to 24 hours. To serve, bake the peppers for 25 to 30 minutes or until heated through. Let the sauce stand at room temperature while peppers bake.

FILLING

  1 **pound ground pork or ground raw turkey or chicken**
⅓ **cup chopped onion (1 small)**
  1 **clove garlic, minced**
  2 **cups chopped peeled apple and/or pear (2 large)**
  1 **8-ounce can tomato sauce**
¼ **cup raisins**
½ **teaspoon salt**
¼ **teaspoon ground cinnamon**
¼ **teaspoon ground cumin**
¼ **cup slivered almonds, toasted**

  6 **large fresh poblano peppers or 3 small green sweet peppers**
  1 **recipe Walnut Sauce Chili Colorado (see recipe, page 28) (optional)**

1. For filling, in a large skillet cook ground pork or other meat, onion, and garlic until meat is brown and onion is tender. Drain off fat. Stir in chopped apple and/or pear, tomato sauce, raisins, salt, cinnamon, and cumin. Bring to boiling. Reduce heat and simmer, covered, for 10 minutes. Stir in almonds.

2. Meanwhile, cut a lengthwise slit in a side of each poblano pepper and remove seeds and membranes. (If using, halve the sweet peppers lengthwise; discard seeds and membranes.) In a saucepan cook poblano peppers or sweet peppers in *boiling water* about 5 minutes or until crisp-tender. Drain the peppers well.

3. Spoon the meat mixture into the peppers. Place the stuffed peppers in a 2-quart rectangular baking dish. Bake in a 350° oven about 20 minutes or until heated through.

4. To serve, spoon Walnut Sauce and, if desired, Chili Colorado onto serving plates. Place stuffed peppers on top of the sauces. Makes 6 servings.

WALNUT SAUCE

In a blender container or food processor bowl, combine ½ cup *walnuts;* one 3-ounce package *cream cheese,* cut up; ⅓ cup *milk;* ¼ teaspoon *ground cinnamon;* and ⅛ teaspoon *salt.* Cover and blend or process until smooth. Makes about 1 cup.

For many Americans, tacos were their introduction to Mexican food. In the United States, tacos are usually crisp, or occasionally soft, corn tortillas folded in half and filled with meat, cheese, lettuce, tomatoes, and other foods. In Mexico, the taco more likely is a warm flour or corn tortilla, wrapped around a cooked filling topped with sauce, and rolled and eaten as is. Depending on where you go in Mexico, tacos may be lightly fried or crisp.

ALL MEXICO

Shredded Pork Tacos
TACOS DE CERDO DESHEBRADO

MAKES 4 TACOS   START TO FINISH: 25 MINUTES

NUTRITION FACTS PER TACO

		Daily Values
Calories	256	12%
Total fat	15 g	23%
Saturated fat	5 g	25%
Cholesterol	67 mg	22%
Sodium	280 mg	11%
Carbohydrate	11 g	3%
Fiber	1 g	2%
Protein	19 g	

4 taco shells or four 6- to 8-inch flour tortillas
1¼ cups Shredded Savory Pork (see recipe, page 45)
¼ cup Picante Sauce (see recipe, page 24) or salsa
1 cup shredded lettuce
¼ cup finely shredded anejo enchilado cheese or Monterey Jack cheese
2 tablespoons sliced pitted ripe olives
Dairy sour cream (optional)
1 medium avocado, halved, seeded, peeled, and chopped (optional)

1. To warm taco shells, place on a baking sheet and heat in a 350° oven for 5 to 7 minutes or until heated through. (Or, to warm flour tortillas, wrap tortillas tightly in foil. Heat in a 350° oven about 10 minutes or until heated through.)

2. Meanwhile, in a medium saucepan combine Shredded Savory Pork and Picante Sauce or salsa; heat through (add additional Picante Sauce or salsa, if necessary, to moisten).

3. To assemble tacos, place pork mixture in warm taco shells. (If using flour tortillas, place pork mixture in center of warm tortillas; fold in half over pork mixture.) Top with lettuce, cheese, and olives. If desired, serve with sour cream and avocado. Makes 4 tacos.

MEXICAN CHEESES

A growing number of American-made Mexican cheeses are now available in supermarkets. The following information and suggested substitutes will help you pick the ones you want.

Asadero (ah-sa-DAY-ro), queso quesadilla (KAY-so kay-sa-DEE-yah), and Chihuahua (chee-WHA-wha) are known for their excellent melting qualities—perfect for quesadillas and any dish where a smooth texture is required. Their flavors are similar to Monterey Jack or Muenster, but the melting characteristics are not.

Anejo enchilado (ah-NAY-ho en-cheel-AH-doe) is a pungent, salty, hard cheese that is excellent grated as a change from cheddar for tacos. Substitute a good fresh grated Parmesan if anejo is unavailable.

Queso fresco (KAY-so FRESK-o), or fresh cheese, is delicious crumbled over salad, refried beans, and *chilaquiles*, a lasagna-type Mexican entrée. Brands vary in texture and saltiness; some resemble ricotta, others feta. Feta can be substituted, but if it's very salty, it may need to be rinsed. Farmer cheese and a dry ricotta are also good substitutes.

REGION: PUEBLA

Pork Chops in Adobo Sauce
CHULETAS DE CERDO EN ADOBO

MAKES 4 SERVINGS   PREP: 1¼ HOURS   COOK: 30 MINUTES

Mexican adobos are chili pastes originally used as marinades and flavored with herbs, sometimes spices, and a bit of vinegar. Our version cooks the pork in the sauce as a time-saver. The mild, smoky taste of the adobo envelops the pork during the relatively short cooking time.

SAUCE
- 3 dried ancho peppers
- 1 medium onion, cut up
- ½ cup tomato sauce
- 2 tablespoons vinegar
- 1 tablespoon all-purpose flour
- ½ teaspoon dried oregano, crushed
- ½ teaspoon dried thyme, crushed
- ¼ teaspoon cumin seed
- ¼ teaspoon salt
- ¼ teaspoon ground black pepper
- 2 cloves garlic, minced

- 4 pork loin chops, cut ½ inch thick
- 4 cups shredded lettuce
  Sliced radishes (optional)
  Sliced onion (optional)

1. For adobo sauce, cut peppers open; discard stems and seeds. Place peppers on a foil-lined baking sheet. Bake in a 375° oven for 6 minutes. Remove from oven; cool. Tear peppers into 2-inch pieces. Place in a small bowl and cover with *boiling water*. Let stand for 45 to 60 minutes to soften. Drain well.

2. In a blender container or food processor bowl, combine drained pepper pieces, onion, tomato sauce, vinegar, flour, oregano, thyme, cumin seed, salt, black pepper, and garlic. Cover and blend or process until nearly smooth. Pour sauce into a large skillet.

3. Trim fat from meat. Place pork chops in sauce, turning once to coat both sides. Simmer chops, covered, over low heat about 30 minutes or until no pink remains in pork and juices run clear.

4. Arrange chops on a lettuce-lined serving platter. Spoon sauce over chops. If desired, garnish with sliced radishes and onion. Makes 4 servings.

LOW-FAT

NUTRITION FACTS PER SERVING		Daily Values
Calories	134	6%
Total fat	5 g	7%
Saturated fat	2 g	8%
Cholesterol	34 mg	11%
Sodium	395 mg	16%
Carbohydrate	10 g	3%
Fiber	3 g	11%
Protein	12 g	

MAKE AHEAD

Prepare the sauce as directed. Cover and chill for up to 3 days or freeze for up to 6 months.

POULTRY

REGION: YUCATAN

Chicken Baked in Banana Leaves

POLLO PIBIL

MAKES 6 SERVINGS	PREP: 20 MINUTES	MARINATE: 8 TO 24 HOURS	BAKE: 1 HOUR

MARINADE
- 1 tablespoon annatto seeds or 1 tablespoon chili powder
- 1 teaspoon whole black pepper
- 4 whole allspice
- ½ teaspoon dried oregano
- ½ teaspoon cumin seed
- 1 teaspoon finely shredded orange peel
- ¾ cup orange juice
- ¼ teaspoon salt
- 2 cloves garlic, minced
- 1 cup chopped onion (1 large)

2½ to 3 pounds meaty chicken pieces (breasts, thighs, and drumsticks)
Banana leaves

PICKLED RED ONIONS
- 1 pound red onions, sliced and separated into rings (about 3½ cups)
- ¼ cup white vinegar
- ½ teaspoon salt
- ½ teaspoon dried oregano, crushed
- ¼ teaspoon whole black pepper
- 2 cloves garlic, minced

1. For marinade, in a blender container or food processor bowl, combine the annatto seeds or chili powder, whole black pepper, allspice, oregano, and cumin seed. Cover; blend or process to a fine powder. Add the orange peel, orange juice, salt, and garlic. Cover; blend or process until nearly smooth. Stir in onion.

2. If desired, skin chicken. Rinse chicken; pat dry. Place chicken in a plastic bag set in a deep bowl. Pour marinade over chicken. Close bag. Marinate in refrigerator 8 to 24 hours, turning bag occasionally.

3. Meanwhile, if using, cut banana leaves into six 12×9-inch rectangles. Loosely roll up the rectangles and place in a steamer basket over, but not touching, *boiling water.* Cover and steam for 20 to 30 minutes or until leaves are soft and pliable.

4. Remove chicken from marinade; discard marinade. Divide chicken pieces among banana leaf rectangles. Wrap banana leaves around each serving of chicken. Overwrap with foil and seal tightly. (If banana leaves are unavailable, wrap chicken in foil rectangles and seal tightly.) Place wrapped chicken pieces in a single layer in a shallow baking pan. Bake in a 375° oven 1 hour or until chicken is tender and no longer pink.

5. Meanwhile, for pickled red onions, place onion rings in a saucepan; cover with *boiling water.* Let stand 1 minute. Drain well. Return onion rings to saucepan; stir in vinegar, salt, oregano, whole black pepper, and garlic. Bring to boiling; reduce heat. Simmer, covered, about 3 minutes or until onions are tender. Remove from heat; transfer to a small mixing bowl. Let stand until cool, stirring occasionally. To serve, remove foil from chicken. Serve chicken in banana leaves along with onions. Makes 6 servings.

Banana leaves are as near as the freezer section in your favorite Hispanic or Asian market. The leaves impart unique aroma and flavor, but if they're unavailable, aluminum foil works for wrapping. The Mayan word pib *refers to a stone-lined barbecue pit, the traditional oven in the Yucatan. Annatto seeds, or* achiote, *the brick red spice and coloring agent found in Hispanic markets, add a distinctive color to the chicken. Annatto also is used as a natural coloring agent in cheddar cheese and butter.*

LOW-FAT

NUTRITION FACTS PER SERVING		
		Daily Values
Calories	243	12%
Total fat	11 g	16%
Saturated fat	3 g	14%
Cholesterol	86 mg	28%
Sodium	179 mg	7%
Carbohydrate	7 g	2%
Fiber	1 g	4%
Protein	29 g	

MAKE AHEAD

Prepare pickled red onions as directed. Cover and chill for up to 2 days. Marinate chicken for 24 hours.

REGION: PUEBLA

Chicken with Mole
POLLO EN MOLE POBLANO

A mole is a complex Mexican sauce that may or may not be spicy, depending upon the chilies used. Although there are many types of mole, one of the most famous is mole poblano. It is said Pueblan nuns created it from native and European ingredients to honor a visiting Spanish viceroy. The spicy red sauce, made richer by a minuscule amount of unsweetened chocolate, usually is served with chicken or turkey.

NUTRITION FACTS PER SERVING

		Daily Values
Calories	314	15%
Total fat	18 g	27%
Saturated fat	4 g	20%
Cholesterol	87 mg	28%
Sodium	336 mg	14%
Carbohydrate	7 g	2%
Fiber	2 g	6%
Protein	31 g	

Make Ahead

Prepare and cook the mole as directed. Cover and chill for up to 2 days. To serve, place the sauce in a small saucepan and heat over medium heat until hot.

MAKES 6 SERVINGS   PREP: 1 HOUR   BAKE: 35 MINUTES

MOLE
    2 **dried ancho, mulato, or pasilla peppers**
 1¼ **cups chicken broth**
    1 **medium tomato, peeled and cut up**
    1 **medium onion, cut up**
   ⅓ **cup slivered almonds, toasted**
   ½ **ounce unsweetened chocolate, cut up**
    2 **cloves garlic, minced**
    1 **tablespoon sugar**
   ½ **teaspoon ground coriander**
   ¼ **teaspoon salt**
   ¼ **teaspoon ground cinnamon**

 2½ **to 3 pounds meaty chicken pieces (breasts, thighs, and drumsticks)**
    1 **tablespoon cooking oil**
    1 **tablespoon sesame seed, toasted (optional)**

1. For mole, cut peppers open; discard stems and seeds. Cut peppers into small pieces. Place in a small bowl and cover with *boiling water*. Let stand for 45 to 60 minutes to soften. Drain well.

2. In a blender container or food processor bowl, combine drained pepper pieces, chicken broth, tomato, onion, almonds, chocolate, garlic, sugar, coriander, salt, and cinnamon. Cover and blend or process until nearly smooth, stopping to scrape sides if necessary.

3. Meanwhile, rinse chicken; pat dry. Arrange chicken in a lightly greased shallow baking pan. Brush with oil. Bake in a 375° oven for 35 to 40 minutes or until chicken is tender and no longer pink. Transfer to a serving platter.

4. Meanwhile, transfer mole to a small saucepan. Bring to boiling. Reduce heat and simmer, uncovered, about 15 minutes or until thickened, stirring frequently. Spoon some of the mole sauce over chicken pieces. If desired, sprinkle with sesame seed. Pass remaining mole. Makes 6 servings.

REGION: CENTRAL MEXICO

Swiss Enchiladas

ENCHILADAS SUIZAS

MAKES 4 SERVINGS   PREP: 1¼ HOURS   BAKE: 20 MINUTES

Enchiladas with cream in the sauce are known as enchiladas suizas. In this case, sour cream mellows the tangy green sauce made with tomatillos. Corn tortillas, softened to make them pliable, are filled with chicken and a mild cumin-flavored cream cheese sauce. A final sprinkling of shredded cheese makes this casserole special enough for company.

SAUCE

- 3 large fresh poblano or Anaheim peppers
- 5 to 6 tomatillos, husked and rinsed, or one 13-ounce can tomatillos, rinsed and drained
- 1 small onion, cut up
- ¼ cup snipped fresh cilantro
- 2 cloves garlic, minced
- ½ cup chicken broth
- 1 teaspoon sugar
- ¼ teaspoon salt
- ⅛ teaspoon ground black pepper
- ½ cup dairy sour cream

- 8 6-inch corn tortillas

FILLING

- ¼ cup chopped onion
- 1 tablespoon margarine or butter
- 1 3-ounce package cream cheese, softened
- 1 tablespoon milk
- ¼ teaspoon ground cumin
- 2 cups chopped cooked chicken or turkey

- ½ cup shredded Chihuahua cheese or Monterey Jack cheese

1. For sauce, to roast fresh poblano or Anaheim peppers, halve peppers lengthwise; remove stems, seeds, and membranes. Place, cut side down, on a foil-lined baking sheet. Bake in a 425° oven for 15 to 20 minutes or until skins are blistered and dark. Remove from baking sheet; immediately cover tightly with foil. Let stand 30 minutes to steam. With a knife, remove skin from peppers, pulling skin off in strips; discard skin. Coarsely chop roasted peppers; set aside.

2. Meanwhile, if using fresh tomatillos, place in a large saucepan; add enough *water* to cover. Bring to boiling. Reduce heat and simmer, covered, for 8 to 10 minutes or until soft; drain.

3. In a blender container or food processor bowl, place roasted peppers, fresh or canned tomatillos, onion, cilantro, and garlic. Cover and blend or process until almost smooth.

4. Transfer sauce to a small saucepan. Stir in chicken broth, sugar, salt, and black pepper. Bring to boiling. Reduce heat and simmer, covered, for 10 minutes; stir in sour cream. Set aside.

5. Wrap tortillas tightly in foil. Heat in a 350° oven about 10 minutes or until heated through.

6. Meanwhile, for filling, cook onion in margarine or butter until tender. Stir in cream cheese, milk, and cumin. Add chicken or turkey; stir until combined. Spoon about ¼ cup of the filling on each tortilla near an end; roll up. Place filled tortillas, seam side down, in a 2-quart rectangular baking dish. Top with sauce. Bake, covered, in a 350° oven for 20 to 25 minutes or until heated through. Remove from oven and sprinkle with shredded cheese. Makes 4 servings.

NUTRITION FACTS PER SERVING

		Daily Values
Calories	519	25%
Total fat	28 g	43%
Saturated fat	14 g	67%
Cholesterol	117 mg	38%
Sodium	570 mg	23%
Carbohydrate	35 g	11%
Fiber	1 g	5%
Protein	33 g	

MAKE AHEAD

Prepare the sauce as directed through Step 3. Cover and chill for up to 2 days.

The key word in this recipe name is verde, *the color green. All the major ingredients—tomatillos, pepitas, green chilies, and cilantro—are green. Each contributes to the fresh, light taste of this quick-to-prepare sauce. Green pumpkin seed moles are based on ancient sauces the Aztecs made before the Spanish conquest.*

REGION: CENTRAL MEXICO

Chicken with Green Pumpkin Seed Mole
POLLO EN MOLE VERDE DE PEPITA

MAKES 4 SERVINGS   START TO FINISH: 25 MINUTES

LOW-FAT

NUTRITION FACTS PER SERVING

		Daily Values
Calories	202	10%
Total fat	7 g	11%
Saturated fat	1 g	7%
Cholesterol	60 mg	19%
Sodium	846 mg	35%
Carbohydrate	11 g	3%
Fiber	3 g	10%
Protein	24 g	

4 skinless, boneless chicken
   breast halves
  Nonstick spray coating

MOLE
½ cup chopped onion
   (1 medium)
1 clove garlic, minced
2 teaspoons cooking oil
1 13-ounce can tomatillos,
   rinsed and drained
⅓ cup shelled raw pumpkin
   seed (pepitas), toasted*
1 4-ounce can diced green chili
   peppers
¼ cup chicken broth
3 tablespoons snipped fresh
   cilantro
¼ teaspoon salt

   Shelled raw pumpkin seed
   (pepitas), toasted*
   (optional)

1. Rinse chicken; pat dry. Spray an unheated large skillet with cooking spray. Cook chicken in skillet over medium heat for 10 to 12 minutes or until tender and no longer pink, turning once. Remove chicken; keep warm.

2. For mole, in the same skillet cook onion and garlic in hot oil about 5 minutes or until onion is tender.

3. In a blender container or food processor bowl, combine onion mixture, tomatillos, toasted pumpkin seed, chili peppers, chicken broth, cilantro, and salt. Cover and blend or process with several on-off turns to a coarse puree. Transfer mole to the skillet and heat through.

4. To serve, spoon mole over chicken breasts. If desired, sprinkle with additional pumpkin seed. Makes 4 servings.

*Note: To toast pumpkin seeds, spread seeds in a shallow baking pan. Bake in a 350° oven about 10 minutes or until toasted. The toasted pumpkin seeds may be kept tightly covered in the refrigerator for 1 week. For longer storage, freeze them, raw or toasted, for up to 1 year.

When large tortillas are filled and rolled tightly into narrow cylinders, they resemble flutes, the musical instrument for which flautas are named. They are then fried to a golden crispness and served with guacamole and sour cream for a nice contrast in texture and temperature.

REGION: NORTHERN MEXICO

flautas

MAKES 6 FLAUTAS   PREP: 25 MINUTES   FRY: 2 MINUTES PER BATCH

NUTRITION FACTS PER FLAUTA

		Daily Values
Calories	539	26%
Total fat	33 g	51%
Saturated fat	5 g	26%
Cholesterol	45 mg	15%
Sodium	478 mg	19%
Carbohydrate	39 g	13%
Fiber	2 g	8%
Protein	22 g	

MAKE AHEAD

Prepare the filling as directed. Cover and chill for up to 24 hours.

6 10-inch flour tortillas

FILLING
½ cup chopped onion (1 medium)
1 clove garlic, minced
1 teaspoon cooking oil
2 cups shredded cooked chicken
1 cup canned black beans, rinsed and drained
½ cup salsa
2 tablespoons snipped fresh cilantro or oregano

Cooking oil
3 cups shredded lettuce
Guacamole (see recipe, page 22) (optional)
Fresh Tomato Salsa (see recipe, page 23) or salsa (optional)
Dairy sour cream (optional)

1. Wrap tortillas tightly in foil. Heat in a 350° oven about 10 minutes or until heated through.

2. Meanwhile, for filling, in a large saucepan cook onion and garlic in the 1 teaspoon hot oil until tender. Stir in chicken, black beans, salsa, and cilantro or oregano.

3. For each flauta, spoon about ½ cup filling near one edge of each warm tortilla. Roll up tortillas as tightly as possible. Secure with wooden toothpicks.

4. In a 12-inch skillet heat 1½ inches of cooking oil to 365°. Fry flautas, 2 or 3 at a time, for 2 to 3 minutes or until crisp and golden brown, turning once. Drain on paper towels. Keep flautas warm in a 300° oven while frying remaining ones.

5. To serve, remove toothpicks. Place flautas atop shredded lettuce. If desired, top with Guacamole, Fresh Tomato Salsa or salsa, and sour cream. Makes 6 flautas.

BAKED FLAUTAS

Prepare as above through Step 3. Place flautas on a large baking sheet and brush with 1 tablespoon *cooking oil.* Bake in a 350° oven for 30 to 40 minutes or until golden brown and heated through. Serve as directed above (323 calories, 12 g total fat).

NEW MEXICO & MEXICO

Chicken with New Mexican-Style Rub
POLLO ADOBADO ESTILO NUEVO MÉXICO

MAKES 4 SERVINGS   PREP: 15 MINUTES   BROIL: 12 MINUTES

RUB
- 1 tablespoon dried oregano
- 1 tablespoon dried thyme
- 1 teaspoon coriander seed
- 1 teaspoon aniseed
- ¼ cup chili powder
- 1 teaspoon paprika
- ½ teaspoon cracked black pepper
- ¼ teaspoon salt

- 4 skinless, boneless chicken breast halves (about 1 pound total)

1. For rub, using a mortar and pestle, grind together the oregano, thyme, coriander seed, and aniseed. Stir in chili powder, paprika, cracked black pepper, and salt.* Set seasoning mixture aside.

2. Rinse chicken; pat dry. With your fingers, gently rub some of the seasoning mixture onto both sides of chicken breast halves.

3. Place chicken on the unheated rack of a broiler pan. Broil 4 to 5 inches from the heat for 12 to 15 minutes or until tender and no longer pink, turning once. (Or, grill on the rack of an uncovered grill directly over medium coals for 12 to 15 minutes or until tender and no longer pink, turning once.) Makes 4 servings.

***Note:** The seasoning rub makes about 7 tablespoons. Store the leftover mixture, covered, in a cool, dry place and use within 6 months.

If you don't own a mortar and pestle—let alone the three-legged molcajete and tejolote—grind the spices and herbs in a coffee or spice grinder. The Spanish, in a bow to their Mediterranean heritage, may have first coated the meat with olive oil before applying the dry mixture. Try this seasoning on pot roast for a slow-roasted meal with Mexican flavor.

LOW-FAT

NUTRITION FACTS PER SERVING

		Daily Values
Calories	123	6%
Total fat	3 g	4%
Saturated fat	1 g	4%
Cholesterol	59 g	19%
Sodium	88 mg	3%
Carbohydrate	0 g	0%
Fiber	0 g	0%
Protein	22 g	

REGION: YUCATAN

*C*hicken and Lime Soup
CALDO DO POLLO CON LIMÓN

MAKES ABOUT 8 CUPS (6 MAIN-DISH SERVINGS)   START TO FINISH: 1¼ HOURS

1 **pound boneless, skinless chicken breast halves**
6 **cups chicken broth**
4 **chicken gizzards* (optional)**
4 **chicken livers* (optional)**
½ **cup chopped onion (1 medium)**
½ **cup chopped green sweet pepper**
1 **clove garlic, minced**
1 **tablespoon cooking oil**
1 **cup chopped tomato (1 large) or one 7½-ounce can tomatoes, cut up**
¾ **teaspoon dried oregano, crushed**
1 **teaspoon grated lime peel**
3 **tablespoons lime juice**
6 **6-inch corn tortillas or 7-inch flour tortillas**
 Nonstick spray coating
 Habanero or jalapeño peppers, rinsed, seeded, and chopped (optional)
 Thin lime slices (optional)

1. Rinse chicken breast halves; pat dry. In a large pot bring chicken broth to boiling. Add chicken breast halves and simmer, covered, about 15 minutes or until tender and no longer pink. Remove chicken from broth. Let stand until cool enough to handle; shred chicken and set aside. Strain broth and set aside. (*If using chicken gizzards and livers, rinse and pat dry. Combine gizzards and chicken broth in a large pot. Bring to boiling. Reduce heat and simmer, covered, for 1 hour. Add chicken breast halves and simmer, covered, for 5 minutes. Add chicken livers and simmer for 5 to 10 minutes more or until chicken breasts and livers are tender. Remove solids from broth. Let stand until cool enough to handle. Finely chop gizzards and livers; shred chicken. Strain broth.)

2. In the same pot cook onion, sweet pepper, and garlic in hot oil until tender. Stir in strained broth, chopped tomato or undrained canned tomatoes, and oregano. Bring to boiling. Stir in lime peel and lime juice. Reduce heat and simmer, covered, for 20 minutes. Stir in shredded chicken and, if using, chopped gizzards and livers; heat through.

3. Meanwhile, cut tortillas in half. Cut crosswise into ½-inch-wide strips. Spray the strips lightly with cooking spray. Arrange the strips in a single layer on a baking sheet. Bake in a 350° oven about 10 minutes or until lightly browned and crisp.

4. To serve, ladle soup into bowls. Top each serving with tortilla strips. If desired, garnish with habanero or jalapeño peppers and lime slices. Makes about 8 cups (6 main-dish servings).

This tangy soup comes from the Yucatan where a special type of lime thrives. The common Persian limes found in every supermarket taste just as delicious. The broth contains a generous amount of chicken, which contrasts well with the crisp tortilla strips. For those who don't enjoy chicken livers and gizzards, simply omit them and enjoy this out-of-the-ordinary soup.

LOW-FAT

NUTRITION FACTS PER SERVING

		Daily Values
Calories	220	10%
Total fat	7 g	10%
Saturated fat	1 g	7%
Cholesterol	41 mg	13%
Sodium	856 mg	35%
Carbohydrate	18 g	5%
Fiber	1 g	2%
Protein	22 g	

MAKE AHEAD

Prepare the soup as directed. Cover and chill for up to 24 hours. To serve, prepare tortilla strips and reheat soup over medium heat until hot.

Be forewarned by the name of this classic Mexican dish and don't serve it on your best table linens. It's inevitable that the rich, red chile sauce will stain as advertised. But don't let that deter you—it's a great meal.

REGION: CENTRAL MEXICO

Tablecloth-Stainer Stew
MANCHAMANTELES

MAKES ABOUT 8 CUPS (6 MAIN-DISH SERVINGS)   PREP: 1¼ HOURS   COOK: 50 MINUTES

MAKE AHEAD

Prepare stew as directed through Step 5. Cover and chill for up to 24 hours. To serve, bring the stew to boiling; reduce heat. Continue with Step 6.

2 to 3 dried ancho peppers
2 to 3 dried pasilla peppers
2½ to 3 pounds meaty chicken pieces (breasts, thighs, and drumsticks)
1 tablespoon cooking oil
½ pound boneless pork shoulder roast or pork blade roast
1 7½-ounce can tomatoes
1 large onion, cut up
3 cloves garlic, minced
1 teaspoon dried oregano, crushed
¼ teaspoon salt
¼ teaspoon ground cinnamon
¼ teaspoon ground black pepper
⅛ teaspoon ground cloves
2 cups chicken broth
1 ripe large plantain or 2 firm medium bananas,* peeled and sliced
1 medium sweet potato, peeled and cut into ½-inch cubes
1 cup thinly sliced, peeled cooking apple (1 medium)
1 cup thinly sliced, peeled pear (1 medium)
1 8-ounce can pineapple chunks (juice pack), drained

1. Cut peppers open; discard stems and seeds. Cut peppers into small pieces. Place in a small bowl and cover with *boiling water*. Let stand 45 to 60 minutes to soften. Drain well; set aside.

2. Meanwhile, skin chicken. Rinse chicken; pat dry. In a 4-quart pot cook chicken in hot oil over medium heat about 10 minutes or until lightly browned, turning to brown evenly.

3. Trim fat from pork; cut into ¾-inch cubes. Remove chicken from pot, reserving drippings in pot. Set chicken aside. Brown pork cubes in drippings in pot. Drain pork well, discarding drippings in pot. Return chicken pieces and pork cubes to pot.

4. In a blender container or food processor bowl, combine drained pepper pieces, undrained tomatoes, onion, garlic, oregano, salt, cinnamon, black pepper, and cloves. Cover and blend or process until smooth.

5. Stir tomato mixture and chicken broth into pot with chicken and pork. Bring to boiling. Stir in plantain (*if using banana, do not add yet). Reduce heat and simmer, covered, over low heat for 20 minutes. Skim off fat. Stir in sweet potato cubes. Cover and simmer about 25 minutes more or until sweet potato is tender.

6. Stir in apple and pear slices. Simmer, covered, for 5 minutes more. Stir in pineapple (if using bananas, add them now). Cover and heat through. Makes about 8 cups (6 main-dish servings).

ALL MEXICO

Chicken and Rice
ARROZ CON POLLO

MAKES 6 SERVINGS   PREP: 20 MINUTES   COOK: 30 MINUTES

2½ to 3 pounds meaty chicken
    pieces (breasts, thighs, and
    drumsticks)
1 tablespoon cooking oil
1¼ cups long-grain rice
1 cup chopped onion (1 large)
2 cloves garlic, minced
2 14½-ounce cans chicken
    broth
1 7½-ounce can tomatoes,
    cut up
2 teaspoons ground cumin
¼ teaspoon ground black
    pepper
    Pinch thread saffron, crushed
    or ⅛ teaspoon ground
    turmeric
1 cup frozen peas

1. Skin chicken; rinse and pat dry. In a 12-inch skillet cook chicken in hot oil over medium heat about 10 minutes or until lightly browned, turning to brown evenly. Remove chicken from skillet, reserving drippings in skillet. Set chicken aside.

2. Add uncooked rice, onion, and garlic to drippings in skillet. Cook and stir over medium heat until rice is lightly browned. Carefully stir in chicken broth, undrained tomatoes, cumin, black pepper, and saffron or turmeric.

3. Place chicken on top of the rice mixture. Bring to boiling. Reduce heat and simmer, covered, for 30 to 35 minutes or until rice is tender and chicken is tender and no longer pink.

4. Remove chicken pieces from skillet; keep warm. Gently stir peas into rice mixture. Let stand for 2 minutes. Transfer rice mixture to a serving platter. Arrange chicken pieces on top of the rice mixture. Makes 6 servings.

Arroz con pollo, the simple casserole of rice and chicken known all over Mexico, has its roots in Spanish paella. Long-grain rice is used in Mexico instead of the classic short-grain rice, but the other ingredients are the same. Luckily, only a few strands of saffron— the most expensive spice—are needed to achieve its famous yellow color and bittersweet flavor. Turmeric may be substituted to achieve a similar color.

NUTRITION FACTS PER SERVING		
		Daily Values
Calories	436	21%
Total fat	14 g	22%
Saturated fat	4 g	17%
Cholesterol	87 mg	28%
Sodium	593 mg	24%
Carbohydrate	39 g	12%
Fiber	2 g	7%
Protein	35 g	

FISH AND SEAFOOD

REGION: VERACRUZ

Snapper Veracruz
HUACHINANGO A LA VERACRUZANA

MAKES 6 SERVINGS   START TO FINISH: 30 MINUTES

1½ **pounds fresh or frozen**
   skinless red snapper or
   other fish fillets
⅛ **teaspoon salt**
⅛ **teaspoon ground black**
   pepper

SAUCE
 1 **large onion, sliced and**
   separated into rings
 2 **cloves garlic, minced**
 1 **tablespoon cooking oil**
 2 **cups chopped tomatoes**
      (2 large)
¼ **cup sliced pimiento-stuffed**
   olives
¼ **cup dry white wine**
 2 **tablespoons capers, drained**
 1 **to 2 fresh jalapeño or serrano**
   peppers, seeded and
   chopped, or 1 to 2 canned
   jalapeño peppers, rinsed,
   drained, seeded, and
   chopped
½ **teaspoon sugar**
 1 **bay leaf**

1½ **pounds potatoes, boiled***
   (optional)

1. Thaw fish, if frozen. Cut fish into 6 serving-size portions. Rinse fish; pat dry. Sprinkle fish fillets with salt and black pepper.

2. For sauce, in a large skillet cook onion and garlic in hot oil until onion is tender. Stir in tomatoes, olives, wine, capers, jalapeño or serrano peppers, sugar, and bay leaf. Bring to boiling. Add fillets to skillet. Return to boiling. Reduce heat and simmer, covered, for 6 to 10 minutes or until fish flakes easily with a fork.

3. Use a slotted spoon to carefully transfer fish from skillet to a serving platter. Cover and keep warm.

4. Boil sauce in skillet for 5 to 6 minutes or until reduced to about 2 cups, stirring occasionally. Remove bay leaf. Spoon sauce over fish. If desired, serve with boiled potatoes.* Makes 6 servings.

*Note: To prepare potatoes, peel skins and remove eyes, sprouts, and green areas. Cut potatoes into quarters. Cook, covered, in a small amount of *boiling salted water* for 20 to 25 minutes or until tender. Drain.

With its location on the Gulf of Mexico, it's no wonder Veracruz is famous for seafood. It was once the only east coast port allowed to operate in New Spain. Snapper Veracruz, one of Mexico's best known fish recipes, is a melding of flavors— Spanish green olives and capers with jalapeño peppers from nearby Jalapa, the capital of the state of Veracruz. To douse the fire from the peppers, this meal typically includes boiled potatoes.

LOW-FAT

NUTRITION FACTS PER SERVING

		Daily Values
Calories	174	8%
Total fat	5 g	7%
Saturated fat	1 g	3%
Cholesterol	42 mg	13%
Sodium	260 mg	10%
Carbohydrate	7 g	2%
Fiber	6 g	5%
Protein	24 g	

This whimsically named fish dish refers to the small amount of alcohol used in the sauce. Tequila is used in central Mexico where the idea originated, but using red wine creates a mild, mellow sauce.

REGION: CENTRAL MEXICO

Drunken Fish

PESCADO BORRACHO

NUTRITION FACTS PER SERVING

		Daily Values
Calories	242	12%
Total fat	9 g	13%
Saturated fat	2 g	7%
Cholesterol	25 mg	8%
Sodium	300 mg	12%
Carbohydrate	11 g	3%
Fiber	4 g	16%
Protein	22 g	

MAKE AHEAD

Prepare the sauce as directed in Steps 2 through 4. Cover and chill for up to 2 days. To serve, place sauce in a covered saucepan and heat over medium heat until hot.

MAKES 4 SERVINGS   PREP: 30 MINUTES   STAND: 45 MINUTES   BAKE: 20 MINUTES

4 fresh or frozen salmon, halibut, or swordfish steaks, cut 1 inch thick (about 1¼ pounds)

SAUCE
3 dried ancho or mulato peppers or 2 to 3 tablespoons chili powder
¼ cup tequila or dry red wine
½ cup chopped onion (1 medium)
2 cloves garlic, minced
1 tablespoon olive oil or cooking oil
2 cups chopped tomatoes (2 large) or one 14½-ounce can diced tomatoes
½ teaspoon dried oregano, crushed
¼ teaspoon salt
¼ teaspoon ground cumin

1 recipe Mexican Rice (see page 74) or 3 cups hot cooked rice (optional)

1. Thaw fish, if frozen. Rinse fish; pat dry. Set aside.

2. Meanwhile, for sauce, if using dried peppers, cut peppers open; discard stems and seeds. Cut the peppers into small pieces. Place in a small bowl and cover with *boiling water*. Let stand 45 to 60 minutes to soften. Drain well.

3. Combine tequila or wine and drained pepper pieces in a blender container or food processor bowl. Cover and blend or process until nearly smooth.

4. In a medium saucepan cook onion and garlic in hot oil until tender. Stir in chopped tomatoes or undrained canned tomatoes, oregano, salt, and cumin. Add blended tequila or wine mixture (if using chili powder, stir it in now). Bring to boiling. Reduce heat and simmer, covered, for 10 minutes.

5. Place fish in a greased 2-quart rectangular baking dish. Spoon about ½ cup of the sauce over fish (cover remaining sauce and keep warm). Bake fish, covered, in a 350° oven about 20 to 25 minutes or until fish flakes easily when tested with a fork.

6. Carefully transfer the fish to a serving platter. Season to taste with *salt* and *ground black pepper*. If desired, serve with Mexican Rice or hot cooked rice. Pass remaining sauce. Makes 4 servings.

TEXAS & NEW MEXICO

Fish in Smoked Pepper Marinade

PESCADO CON PIMIENTO MORRÓN AL MESQUITE

Some like it hot, and for those who do, this marinade is for you. Quickly made from canned chipotle peppers in adobo sauce, the marinade gives a hot, smoky tang to grilled firm-fleshed fish such as halibut, swordfish, and even shark. Or, serve the marinade heated as a taco or enchilada sauce.

MAKES 6 SERVINGS   PREP: 15 MINUTES   MARINATE: 30 MINUTES   BROIL: 8 MINUTES

1½ **pounds fresh or frozen halibut, swordfish, or shark steaks, about 1 inch thick**

MARINADE
1 **to 2 canned chipotle peppers in adobo sauce**
1 **cup chopped red sweet pepper**
2 **tablespoons lime juice**
2 **cloves garlic, minced**
1 **8-ounce can tomato sauce**
⅛ **teaspoon ground black pepper**

1. Thaw fish, if frozen. Rinse fish; pat dry with paper towels. Cut into 6 serving-size pieces, if necessary. Set aside.

2. For marinade, drain canned chipotle pepper(s), reserving *1 tablespoon* of the adobo sauce. If desired, cut chipotle pepper(s) open and scrape out seeds.

3. In a blender container or food processor bowl, combine chipotle peppers, reserved adobo sauce, sweet pepper, lime juice, and garlic. Cover and blend or process until smooth. Add tomato sauce and black pepper. Cover and blend or process just until combined. Pour about half of the marinade into a shallow dish.

4. Add fish steaks to dish; spoon remaining marinade over fish. Cover and marinate at room temperature for 30 minutes.

5. Using a wide spatula, lift fish with marinade to the greased, unheated rack of a broiler pan. Broil 4 inches from the heat for 5 minutes. Carefully turn fish over. Broil 3 to 7 minutes more or until fish flakes easily with a fork. Discard any remaining marinade. (Or, place fish in a well-greased wire grill basket. Grill on the rack of an uncovered grill directly over medium coals for 8 to 12 minutes or just until fish begins to flake easily, turning once.) Makes 6 servings.

LOW-FAT

NUTRITION FACTS PER SERVING

		Daily Values
Calories	133	6%
Total fat	3 g	4%
Saturated fat	.4 g	1%
Cholesterol	36 mg	12%
Sodium	208 mg	8%
Carbohydrate	2 g	0%
Fiber	.4 g	1%
Protein	24 g	

Baja Mexico has its own deep-fried fish tacos that are coated with batter. A healthier grilled version is served in the Yucatan. Don't marinate longer than 30 minutes or the citrus juice will begin to cook the fish. Try catfish, salmon, sea bass, halibut, tuna, or any fresh fish you prefer. Serve with tropical fruits or Mango Salsa (see recipe, page 29) to lend the tacos even more flavors from the Yucatan.

REGION: YUCATAN

fish Tacos
TACOS DE PESCADO

MAKES 4 SERVINGS   PREP: 20 MINUTES   MARINATE: 30 MINUTES   BROIL: 8 MINUTES

NUTRITION FACTS PER SERVING

		Daily Values
Calories	373	18%
Total fat	6 g	9%
Saturated fat	1 g	4%
Cholesterol	43 mg	14%
Sodium	400 mg	16%
Carbohydrate	46 g	15%
Fiber	1 g	5%
Protein	15 g	

1 pound fresh or frozen firm-fleshed fish fillets, cut 1 inch thick

MARINADE
¼ cup tequila
2 tablespoons lime juice or lemon juice
1 fresh jalapeño or serrano pepper, seeded and finely chopped
¼ teaspoon ground cumin
2 cloves garlic, minced

8 8-inch flour tortillas
1½ cups shredded lettuce
1 cup chopped red or green sweet pepper
1 medium red onion, halved and thinly sliced
Snipped fresh cilantro (optional)
Mango or papaya slices (optional)
Salsa (optional)

1. Thaw fish, if frozen. Rinse fish; pat dry. Place fish in a shallow nonmetal dish.

2. For marinade, in a small bowl stir together tequila, lime juice or lemon juice, jalapeño or serrano pepper, cumin, and garlic. Pour marinade over fish. Cover and marinate at room temperature for 30 minutes, turning fish occasionally.

3. Meanwhile, wrap tortillas tightly in foil. Heat in a 350° oven about 10 minutes or until heated through.

4. Drain fish; discard marinade. Pat fish dry.

5. Place fish on the greased unheated rack of a broiler pan. Broil 4 inches from the heat for 5 minutes. Using a wide spatula, carefully turn over the fish. Broil for 3 to 7 minutes more or just until fish flakes easily with a fork. (Or, place fish fillets in a well-greased wire grill basket. Grill on the rack of an uncovered grill directly over medium coals for 8 to 12 minutes or just until fish flakes easily with a fork, turning once.)

6. With a fork, break grilled fish into ½-inch chunks. To assemble tacos, place lettuce in the center of each warm tortilla. Divide fish chunks, sweet pepper, and red onion among tortillas. Fold tortillas in half over filling. If desired, serve tacos with cilantro, mango or papaya slices, and salsa. Makes 4 servings.

Elegance is a simple white bean soup crowned with crabmeat. For this delicious chowder, the only work required is chopping. Although bean soup is common in Mexico, black beans are used more frequently. White beans, as in this Tex-Mex recipe, are traditionally reserved for special occasions.

LOW-FAT

NUTRITION FACTS PER SERVING

		Daily Values
Calories	302	15%
Total fat	7 g	11%
Saturated fat	2 g	11%
Cholesterol	43 mg	14%
Sodium	864 mg	36%
Carbohydrate	38 g	12%
Fiber	1 g	4%
Protein	22 g	

Make Ahead

Prepare the chowder as directed. Cover and chill for up to 2 days. To serve, place in a covered saucepan and reheat over medium heat until hot.

TEXAS & MEXICO

Crab and White Bean Chowder
CREMA DE JAIBA Y FRIJOLES CANARIOS

MAKES 6 CUPS (4 MAIN-DISH SERVINGS)   START TO FINISH: 30 MINUTES

1 large red or green sweet pepper, chopped
1 cup chopped onion (1 large)
1 large fresh Anaheim or poblano pepper, seeded and finely chopped, or one 4-ounce can diced green chili peppers, drained
1 tablespoon olive oil or cooking oil
1 15-ounce can navy beans or great northern beans, rinsed and drained
1 cup chicken broth
2 cups milk
2 tablespoons all-purpose flour
1 6-ounce package frozen crabmeat, thawed and flaked; or one 6½-ounce can crabmeat, drained, flaked, and cartilage removed; or 1 cup chopped cooked chicken
2 tablespoons snipped fresh cilantro
1 tablespoon snipped fresh thyme or ½ teaspoon dried thyme, crushed
Cilantro sprigs (optional)
Chopped red sweet pepper (optional)
Warm tortillas (optional)

1. In a large saucepan cook sweet pepper, onion, and fresh Anaheim or poblano pepper (if using) in hot oil about 3 minutes or until tender. Stir in beans and chicken broth. Bring to boiling. Reduce heat and simmer, covered, for 10 minutes.

2. Stir *½ cup* of the milk into the flour. Add to saucepan along with remaining milk. Cook and stir until slightly thickened and bubbly. Cook and stir 1 minute more. Stir in crabmeat or chicken, cilantro, and thyme (if using canned chili peppers, add them now); heat through.

3. If desired, garnish chowder with additional cilantro and sweet pepper and serve with warm tortillas. Makes about 6 cups (4 main-dish servings).

REGION: WESTERN MEXICO

Seafood Enchiladas

ENCHILADAS DE MARISCOS

MAKES 10 ENCHILADAS   PREP: 1¼ HOURS   BAKE: 25 MINUTES

FILLING
- 2 to 3 dried ancho or mulato peppers
- 2 cups shredded Chihuahua cheese, Monterey Jack cheese, or farmer cheese
- 12 ounces chopped cooked shrimp* or cooked crabmeat; or two 6-ounce packages frozen peeled cooked shrimp, thawed and chopped; or two 6-ounce packages frozen crabmeat, thawed and flaked

- 10 6-inch corn tortillas

SAUCE
- ½ cup chopped onion (1 medium)
- 1 tablespoon olive oil or cooking oil
- ⅓ cup all-purpose flour
- ¼ teaspoon salt
- ¼ teaspoon ground black pepper
- 3 cups milk

1. For filling, cut peppers open; discard stems and seeds. Cut one of the peppers into thin slivers. Cut remaining pepper(s) into small pieces. Place pepper slivers and pieces separately in 2 small bowls. Cover with *boiling water*. Let stand 45 to 60 minutes to soften. Drain well. Set pepper slivers aside to use as a garnish.

2. In a medium mixing bowl combine *1½ cups* of the cheese, the shrimp or crabmeat, and the pepper pieces. Set filling aside.

3. Wrap tortillas tightly in foil. Heat in a 350° oven about 10 minutes or until heated through.

4. Spoon about ¼ cup of the filling on each tortilla near one end; roll up. Place the filled tortillas, seam side down, in a 2-quart rectangular baking dish.

5. For sauce, in a medium saucepan cook onion in hot oil until tender. Stir in flour, salt, and black pepper. Add milk all at once. Cook and stir until thickened and bubbly. Pour sauce over tortillas.

6. Bake, covered, in a 350° oven about 20 minutes or until heated through. Remove foil and sprinkle with remaining cheese. Place pepper slivers diagonally over enchiladas. Return to oven and bake about 5 minutes more or until cheese melts. Makes 10 enchiladas.

*Note: For 12 ounces cooked shrimp, purchase 1½ pounds raw shrimp in the shell. Peel and devein shrimp; rinse well. Simmer, uncovered, in 5 cups *water* and ½ teaspoon *salt* for 1 to 3 minutes or until shrimp turn pink, stirring occasionally. Rinse under cold water. Drain.

Culinary Spanish loosely defines enchiladas as stuffed corn tortillas seasoned with chile. Tortillas are typically softened in a hot chile sauce, filled, rolled, and served immediately. Along the west coast of Mexico, abundant seafood is a logical filling for enchiladas. Since a strong chile sauce would overpower the delicate flavors of seafood, a basic white sauce is substituted and sprinkled with strips of peppers—mild or hot.

NUTRITION FACTS PER ENCHILADA		
		Daily Values
Calories	241	12%
Total fat	11 g	16%
Saturated fat	6 g	27%
Cholesterol	92 mg	30%
Sodium	334 mg	13%
Carbohydrate	19 g	6%
Fiber	.4 g	1%
Protein	17 g	

MAKE AHEAD

Prepare filling as directed. Cover and chill for up to 24 hours.

On the Mexican coasts, fresh seafood often replaces the meat or poultry used in other regions. Shrimp is particularly pleasing with this lively cilantro sauce. Serve it with rice to help quell the heat of the jalapeños or serranos.

REGIONS: WESTERN MEXICO & YUCATAN

Shrimp in Cilantro Sauce
PESCADO EN SALSA DE CILANTRO

MAKES 4 SERVINGS   START TO FINISH: 30 MINUTES

NUTRITION FACTS PER SERVING

		Daily Values
Calories	119	5%
Total fat	5 g	7%
Saturated fat	1 g	3%
Cholesterol	131 mg	43%
Sodium	252 mg	10%
Carbohydrate	4 g	1%
Fiber	.4 g	1%
Protein	15 g	

MAKE AHEAD

Prepare the sauce as directed in Steps 2 and 3, except do not return the sauce to the skillet. Cover and chill the sauce for up to 2 days. To serve, place in a covered saucepan and heat over medium heat until hot.

1 **pound fresh or frozen large shrimp in shells**

SAUCE
4 **to 5 tomatillos, husked, rinsed, and chopped (1 cup)**
½ **cup chopped onion (1 medium)**
2 **cloves garlic, minced**
1 **to 2 fresh jalapeño or serrano peppers, seeded and finely chopped**
1 **tablespoon olive oil or cooking oil**
½ **cup chicken broth**
½ **cup lightly packed fresh cilantro sprigs**
½ **cup lightly packed fresh parsley sprigs**

3 **cups hot cooked rice**
  Tomato wedges (optional)
  Cilantro sprigs (optional)

1. Thaw shrimp, if frozen. Peel and devein shrimp; rinse and pat dry. Set shrimp aside.

2. For green sauce, in a large skillet cook tomatillos, onion, garlic, and jalapeño or serrano pepper in hot oil for about 5 minutes or until onion is tender. Cool slightly.

3. Place tomatillo mixture in a blender container or food processor bowl; add chicken broth, cilantro, and parsley. Cover and blend or process until nearly smooth. Return mixture to skillet and heat through.

4. Meanwhile, in a large saucepan cook shrimp in *boiling water* for 1 to 3 minutes or until shrimp turn pink. Drain well. Toss cooked shrimp with sauce.

5. To serve, spoon shrimp mixture over rice. If desired, garnish with tomato wedges and additional cilantro. Makes 4 servings.

TOMATILLOS

Tomatillos are small, pale green fruits covered with a thin, papery husk that's removed before using. Although not related to the tomato, their texture and appearance is similar to a green tomato. The flavor of the tomatillo is acidic with a hint of lemon and apple. Fresh tomatillos are increasingly available in the produce section of supermarkets. They also are available canned.

RICE, BEANS, AND EGGS

ALL MEXICO

Dry Soup
SOPA SECA

MAKES 6 CUPS (8 SIDE-DISH OR 4 MAIN-DISH SERVINGS)   START TO FINISH: 40 MINUTES

1 cup long-grain rice
1 tablespoon cooking oil
1 cup chopped tomato (1 large)
½ cup chopped onion
    (1 medium)
½ teaspoon chili powder
2 cloves garlic, minced
2½ cups chicken broth
3 tablespoons snipped fresh
    cilantro or parsley
1½ cups shredded cooked
    chicken, beef, or pork
½ cup frozen peas, thawed

1. In a large skillet cook and stir the long-grain rice constantly in hot oil over medium-high heat for 2 to 3 minutes or until rice is lightly browned. Stir in tomato, onion, chili powder, and garlic. Cook and stir for 1 minute more.

2. Carefully stir in chicken broth and cilantro or parsley. Bring to boiling. Reduce heat and simmer, covered, about 20 minutes or until rice is tender and liquid is absorbed.

3. Stir in shredded chicken, beef, or pork and peas. Cover and let stand 5 minutes. Makes 6 cups (8 side-dish or 4 main-dish servings).

Sopa seca literally means dry soup. It is not served dry, but refers to the difference between courses in the traditional five-course comida, *or main meal of the day. Liquid soup* (sopa aquada) *is the first course, and the second course is sopa seca, which is somewhat similar to the pasta course in Italian meals. In fact, it could be a dish of pasta, or even tamales, but is most often rice.*

NUTRITION FACTS
PER SIDE-DISH SERVING

		Daily Values
Calories	194	9%
Total fat	6 g	8%
Saturated fat	1 g	6%
Cholesterol	22 mg	7%
Sodium	278 mg	11%
Carbohydrate	23 g	7%
Fiber	1 g	5%
Protein	12 g	

CILANTRO

Cilantro, also called Chinese parsley, is the small, green leaf of the coriander plant. The leaf may resemble parsley, but cilantro is quite different. Its pungent, musty odor and taste make cilantro an herb people are passionate about—one way or the other. Parsley can be substituted if you or your guests object to the taste. If fresh cilantro is not available, you may find dried leaves in your grocer's spice aisle. To substitute, use about one-third the amount of dried cilantro as fresh.

MAKE AHEAD

Prepare the recipe as directed. Cover and chill up to 24 hours. To serve, place in a covered saucepan with 2 tablespoons water. Heat over medium-low heat for 10 to 15 minutes or until heated through, stirring occasionally.

The standard restaurant version of Mexican rice, often mistakenly called Spanish rice, bears little resemblance to the dish enjoyed at the Mexican table. Vegetables such as carrots and zucchini are sometimes added for extra flavor, texture, and nutrition.

REGION: CENTRAL MEXICO

Mexican Rice
ARROZ A LA MEXICANA

MAKES 3½ CUPS (4 SIDE-DISH SERVINGS)   START TO FINISH: 30 MINUTES

LOW-FAT

NUTRITION FACTS PER SERVING

		Daily Values
Calories	206	10%
Total fat	5 g	7%
Saturated fat	1 g	3%
Cholesterol	0 mg	0%
Sodium	393 mg	16%
Carbohydrate	37 g	12%
Fiber	3 g	13%
Protein	5 g	

MAKE AHEAD

Prepare the recipe as directed. Cover and chill for up to 24 hours. To serve, place in a covered saucepan with 2 tablespoons water. Heat over medium-low heat for 10 to 15 minutes or until heated through, stirring occasionally.

½ cup chopped red onion
   (1 medium)
2 tablespoons medium-hot
   chili powder
1 teaspoon dried oregano,
   crushed
2 cloves garlic, minced
1 tablespoon olive oil or
   cooking oil
¾ cup long-grain rice
1 14½-ounce can beef broth or
   chicken broth
½ cup chopped carrot
1 cup chopped tomato (1 large)
½ cup chopped zucchini
2 tablespoons snipped fresh
   cilantro or parsley

1. In a large skillet cook onion, chili powder, oregano, and garlic in hot oil for 3 minutes. Stir in rice. Cook and stir constantly over medium-high heat about 2 minutes or until rice is lightly browned.

2. Carefully stir in broth and carrot. Bring to boiling. Reduce heat and simmer, covered, for 10 minutes.

3. Stir in the tomato, zucchini, and cilantro or parsley. Cook, covered, for 5 to 10 minutes more or until rice is tender and liquid is absorbed. Makes 3½ cups (4 side-dish servings).

REGION: CENTRAL MEXICO

Pureed corn is used to achieve the creaminess in this unusual rice dish. The poblano peppers add their mild flavor to those of the other vegetables. To spice up this rice dish, serve with your favorite salsa.

Poblano Rice with Vegetables

ARROZ POBLANO CON VERDURAS

MAKES 5 CUPS (6 SIDE-DISH SERVINGS)   PREP: 1 HOUR (IF USING FRESH PEPPERS)   COOK: 25 MINUTES

2 **fresh poblano or Anaheim peppers or one 4-ounce can diced green chili peppers, drained**
1½ **cups frozen whole kernel corn**
⅓ **cup milk**
1 **cup long-grain rice**
2 **teaspoons cooking oil**
2 **cups chicken broth**
1 **cup chopped onion (1 large)**
1 **cup chopped chayote or zucchini (1 medium)**
½ **cup finely chopped carrot**
1 **clove garlic, minced**
1 **bay leaf**

1. If using fresh poblano or Anaheim peppers, halve them lengthwise; remove stems, seeds, and membranes. Place peppers, cut side down, on a foil-lined baking sheet. Bake in a 425° oven for about 20 minutes or until skins are blistered and dark. Remove from baking sheet; immediately cover tightly with foil. Let stand 30 minutes to steam. With a knife, remove skin from peppers, pulling off in strips; discard skin. Finely chop roasted peppers.

2. Meanwhile, rinse the corn in cool water to partially thaw; drain well. Place corn and milk in a blender container or food processor bowl. Cover and blend or process until nearly smooth. Set the corn mixture aside.

3. In a large skillet cook and stir rice in hot oil over medium-high heat for 2 to 3 minutes or until rice is lightly browned.

4. Carefully stir in chopped roasted peppers or canned chili peppers, corn puree, chicken broth, onion, chayote or zucchini, carrot, garlic, and bay leaf. Bring to boiling. Reduce heat and simmer, covered, about 20 minutes or until rice is tender and liquid is absorbed. Remove bay leaf. Makes 5 cups (6 side-dish servings).

LOW-FAT

NUTRITION FACTS PER SERVING

		Daily Values
Calories	211	10%
Total fat	3 g	4%
Saturated fat	1 g	3%
Cholesterol	1 mg	0%
Sodium	279 mg	11%
Carbohydrate	42 g	13%
Fiber	2 g	8%
Protein	7 g	

MAKE AHEAD

Prepare the recipe as directed. Cover and chill for up to 24 hours. To serve, place in a covered saucepan with 2 tablespoons water. Heat over medium-low heat for 10 to 15 minutes or until heated through, stirring occasionally.

*Burritos are Mexican or
Tex-Mex sandwiches that
originally were filled
with refried beans. Now
they are large flour
tortillas wrapped around
a variety of fillings.*

Bean Burritos

BURRITOS DE FRIJOLES

NUTRITION FACTS PER BURRITO		
Calories	466	23%
Total fat	17 g	26%
Saturated fat	6 g	27%
Cholesterol	17 mg	5%
Sodium	562 mg	23%
Carbohydrate	62 g	20%
Fiber	5 g	19%
Protein	18 g	

MAKE AHEAD

Prepare burritos as
directed through Step 5,
except do not add
chopped tomato to
filling. Wrap each
burrito in foil and place
in a freezer container.
Freeze for up to
3 months. To reheat,
place frozen burritos,
loosely wrapped in foil,
on a baking sheet and
heat in a 350° oven
about 30 minutes. Open
foil and bake for 10 to
15 minutes more or
until heated through.

MAKES 6 MAIN-DISH SERVINGS   PREP: 30 MINUTES   STAND: 1 HOUR   COOK: 1½ HOURS   BAKE: 15 MINUTES

1¼ cups dry pinto beans
½ cup chopped onion
    (1 medium)
 2 cloves garlic, minced
 1 tablespoon cooking oil
½ teaspoon salt
 1 recipe 8-inch Spinach
    Tortillas (see page 20) or
    twelve 7- or 8-inch flour
    tortillas
 1 cup shredded Monterey Jack
    cheese or cheddar cheese
¾ cup chopped tomato
    (1 medium)
 1 ripe medium avocado,
    halved, seeded, peeled,
    and chopped (optional)
 Chopped tomato (optional)
 Salsa (optional)

1. Rinse beans. In a large saucepan combine beans
and 4 cups *water*. Bring to boiling. Reduce heat and
simmer for 2 minutes. Remove from heat. Cover and
let stand 1 hour. Drain and rinse beans.

2. Return beans to saucepan. Add 4 cups *fresh water*.
Bring to boiling. Reduce heat and simmer, covered,
about 1½ hours or until beans are very tender. Drain
beans, reserving cooking liquid.

3. For filling, in a large, heavy skillet cook onion and
garlic in hot oil until tender. Remove from heat. Stir
in drained beans and salt. Mash bean mixture,
adding reserved cooking liquid (about ⅓ cup) to
obtain desired consistency.

4. Meanwhile, wrap tortillas tightly in foil. Heat in a
350° oven about 10 minutes or until heated through.

5. To assemble each burrito, spoon a scant ½ cup of
the filling onto each tortilla just below center. Top
with cheese and chopped tomato. Fold edge nearest
filling up and over just until filling is covered. Fold
in 2 adjacent sides just until they meet; roll up.

6. Arrange burritos, seam side down, on a baking
sheet. Bake, covered, in 350° oven for 10 minutes.
Uncover and bake for 5 minutes more.

7. If desired, serve burritos with chopped avocado,
additional chopped tomato, and salsa. Makes
6 main-dish servings.

REGION: OAXACA

*O*axacan Rice and Beans
MOROS Y CRISTIANOS A LA OAXAQUEÑA

MAKES 5 CUPS (6 SIDE-DISH OR 3 MAIN-DISH SERVINGS)   PREP: 25 MINUTES   COOK: 25 MINUTES

A serving of black beans on top of white rice with carrots and green beans makes an attractive, tasty, and nourishing accompaniment to any Mexican meal. The contrasting flavors of the two types of peppers balance out their hotness. (See the photograph on the cover.)

LOW-FAT

NUTRITION FACTS
PER SIDE-DISH SERVING

		Daily Values
Calories	206	10%
Total fat	3 g	4%
Saturated fat	1 g	2%
Cholesterol	0 mg	0%
Sodium	393 mg	16%
Carbohydrate	37 g	12%
Fiber	2 g	9%
Protein	7 g	

*M*AKE AHEAD

Prepare the recipe as directed. Cover and chill for up to 24 hours. To serve, place in a covered saucepan with 2 tablespoons water. Heat over medium-low heat for 10 to 15 minutes or until heated through, stirring occasionally.

½ cup finely chopped carrot
½ cup chopped onion
    (1 medium)
1 fresh poblano pepper, seeded and finely chopped, or one 4-ounce can chopped green chili peppers, drained
1 fresh serrano or jalapeño pepper, seeded and finely chopped, or 1 canned jalapeño pepper, rinsed, drained, seeded, and finely chopped
2 cloves garlic, minced
1 tablespoon cooking oil
1 cup long-grain rice
2¼ cups chicken broth or vegetable broth
1 cup frozen cut green beans, thawed
¼ teaspoon salt
1 cup canned black beans, rinsed and drained, or cooked black beans*

1. In a large skillet cook carrot, onion, poblano pepper or canned chili peppers, serrano or jalapeño pepper, and garlic in hot oil for 3 minutes. Stir in the rice. Cook and stir constantly over medium-high heat for about 2 to 3 minutes or until rice is lightly browned.

2. Carefully stir in chicken or vegetable broth, green beans, and salt. Bring to boiling. Reduce heat and simmer, covered, about 20 minutes or until rice is tender and liquid is absorbed. Stir in black beans; heat through. Makes 5 cups (6 side-dish or 3 main-dish servings).

*Note: For cooked beans, follow Steps 1 and 2 for Bean Burritos on page 76. Use 2 ounces (⅓ cup) dried black beans.

NEW MEXICO

In a hurry? Cut the total preparation and cooking time for this recipe to 30 minutes by using a canned chipotle pepper and canned beans. Rinse and drain the beans to remove excess sodium contained in the liquid.

*B*lack and White Beans with Sweet Peppers

FRIJOLES NEGROS Y CANARIOS CON PIMIENTO MORRÓN

MAKES 3 CUPS (6 SIDE-DISH OR 3 MAIN-DISH SERVINGS)   START TO FINISH: 1 HOUR (PLUS COOKING BEANS*)

1 dried chipotle or ancho pepper or one canned chipotle pepper in adobo sauce, rinsed, drained, seeded, and finely chopped
1 slice bacon
1 cup chopped red or yellow sweet pepper
½ cup chopped green sweet pepper
2 cloves garlic, minced
1½ cups cooked great northern beans* or one 15-ounce can great northern beans, rinsed and drained
1½ cups cooked black beans* or one 15-ounce can black beans, rinsed and drained
¼ cup water
¼ cup snipped fresh cilantro or parsley
¼ teaspoon salt
½ cup shredded asadero cheese or farmer cheese

1. If using dried chipotle or ancho pepper, cut open; discard stem and seeds. Cut pepper into small pieces. Place in a small bowl and cover with *boiling water*. Let stand 45 to 60 minutes to soften. Drain well.

2. Meanwhile, in a large skillet cook bacon over medium heat until crisp. Drain fat, reserving *2 teaspoons* in skillet. Crumble bacon; set aside.

3. Cook sweet peppers and garlic in reserved drippings until tender. Stir in crumbled bacon, chipotle or ancho pepper, great northern beans, black beans, water, cilantro or parsley, and salt. Cook and stir for 10 minutes. (Add additional *water*, if necessary, to reach desired consistency.)

4. Remove from heat and sprinkle cheese over bean mixture. Cover and let stand about 5 minutes or until cheese melts. Makes 3 cups (6 side-dish or 3 main-dish servings).

*Note: For cooked beans, follow Steps 1 and 2 for Bean Burritos on page 76. Use 3 ounces (½ cup) dried great northern beans and 3 ounces (½ cup) dried black beans; cook together in same saucepan.

LOW-FAT

NUTRITION FACTS
PER SIDE-DISH SERVING

		Daily Values
Calories	153	7%
Total fat	3 g	4%
Saturated fat	2 g	8%
Cholesterol	9 mg	3%
Sodium	256 mg	10%
Carbohydrate	22 g	7%
Fiber	5 g	19%
Protein	10 g	

*M*AKE AHEAD

Prepare the recipe as directed through Step 3. Cover and chill for up to 24 hours. To serve, place in a covered saucepan with 2 tablespoons water. Heat over medium-low heat for 10 to 15 minutes or until heated through, stirring occasionally. Continue with Step 4.

This soup is comfort food on a cold, rainy day. It's easy to put together after work, thanks to the convenience of canned beans. Or you can prepare the soup in a crockery cooker and be greeted by its aroma when you get home. Heat corn tortillas and serve with Sangria (see recipe, page 14) for a taste of old Mexico.

LOW-FAT

NUTRITION FACTS
PER SIDE-DISH SERVING

		Daily Values
Calories	173	8%
Total fat	4 g	5%
Saturated fat	.4 g	2%
Cholesterol	0 mg	0%
Sodium	706 mg	29%
Carbohydrate	31g	10%
Fiber	10g	38%
Protein	13g	

MAKE AHEAD

Prepare soup as directed. Cover and chill for up to 24 hours or freeze up to 2 months. To serve, place in a covered saucepan. Heat over medium-low heat for 10 to 15 minutes for chilled soup or about 50 minutes for frozen soup. Heat through, stirring occasionally.

REGIONS: SOUTHERN MEXICO & OAXACA

Black Bean Soup
FRIJOLES NEGROS

MAKES 5½ CUPS (5 SIDE-DISH OR 3 MAIN-DISH SERVINGS)   START TO FINISH: 1¼ HOURS

1 dried poblano, ancho, or chipotle pepper
1 cup chopped green sweet pepper
1 cup chopped onion (1 large)
2 cloves garlic, minced
1 tablespoon olive oil or cooking oil
2 15-ounce cans black beans, rinsed and drained
1 14½-ounce can beef broth
1 cup chopped tomato (1 large)
2 tablespoons snipped fresh cilantro or parsley
1 tablespoon snipped fresh thyme or 1 teaspoon dried thyme, crushed
2 teaspoons snipped fresh oregano or ½ teaspoon dried oregano, crushed
Dairy sour cream (optional)
Fresh cilantro sprigs (optional)

1. Cut dried pepper open; discard stem and seeds. Cut pepper into small pieces. Place in a small bowl and cover with *boiling water*. Let stand 45 to 60 minutes to soften. Drain well.

2. In a large saucepan cook sweet pepper, onion, and garlic in hot oil for 3 minutes. Stir in dried pepper pieces, black beans, beef broth, tomato, cilantro or parsley, thyme, and oregano. Bring to boiling. Reduce heat and simmer, covered, for 30 minutes.

3. If desired, mash beans slightly* and serve soup garnished with sour cream and cilantro. Makes 5½ cups (5 side-dish or 3 main-dish servings).

*Note: For a pureed bean soup, cool soup slightly. Place half of the soup in a food processor bowl or blender container. Cover and process or blend until smooth. Repeat with remaining soup.

CROCKERY-COOKER DIRECTIONS

Prepare dried pepper as above. Omit cooking oil. In a 3½- or 4-quart electric crockery cooker, combine dried pepper pieces, sweet pepper, onion, garlic, black beans, beef broth, tomato, cilantro, thyme, and oregano. Cover and cook on low-heat setting for 8 to 10 hours or on high-heat setting for 4 to 5 hours.

REGION: CENTRAL MEXICO

Lentil Soup
SOPA DE LENTEJAS

The lentil is an often overlooked member of the legume family. This valuable source of vegetable protein has a beanlike texture and a mild, nutty taste, making it a natural for a hearty soup like this one flavored with cumin and cilantro.

MAKES 7½ CUPS (6 SIDE-DISH OR 4 MAIN-DISH SERVINGS)   PREP: 20 MINUTES   COOK: 25 MINUTES

1 slice bacon
1 cup chopped onion (1 large)
2 cloves garlic, minced
½ teaspoon ground cumin
4 cups chicken broth
3 cups water
1¼ cups dry lentils (8 ounces), rinsed and drained
2 tablespoons snipped fresh cilantro
½ teaspoon ground black pepper
1 bay leaf
2 hard-cooked eggs, chopped (optional)

1. In a large saucepan cook bacon over medium heat until crisp. Drain fat, reserving *2 teaspoons* in the saucepan. Crumble bacon; set aside.

2. Cook onion, garlic, and cumin in reserved drippings until onion is tender. Stir in crumbled bacon, chicken broth, water, lentils, cilantro, black pepper, and bay leaf. Bring to boiling. Reduce heat and simmer, covered, for 20 to 30 minutes or until lentils are tender. Remove bay leaf. Mash lentils slightly.

3. If desired, serve soup topped with egg. Makes 7½ cups (6 side-dish or 4 main-dish servings).

LOW-FAT

NUTRITION FACTS
PER SIDE-DISH SERVING

		Daily Values
Calories	174	8%
Total fat	2 g	3%
Saturated fat	1 g	2%
Cholesterol	2 mg	0%
Sodium	542 mg	22%
Carbohydrate	26 g	8%
Fiber	2 g	6%
Protein	14 g	

MAKE AHEAD

Prepare soup as directed. Cover and chill for up to 24 hours. To serve, place in a covered saucepan. Heat over medium-low heat about 15 minutes or until heated through, stirring occasionally.

Your family will never again complain about the same old scrambled eggs when you surprise them with this unusual brunch dish featuring cactus pads. If you're unable to buy cactus in the supermarket or Latin American market, substitute zucchini strips.

REGION: CENTRAL MEXICO

Scrambled Eggs with Cactus
HUEVOS REVUELTOS CON NOPALITOS

MAKES 6 SERVINGS   START TO FINISH: 35 MINUTES

NUTRITION FACTS PER SERVING

		Daily Values
Calories	139	6%
Total fat	9 g	13%
Saturated fat	3 g	12%
Cholesterol	285 mg	94%
Sodium	205 mg	8%
Carbohydrate	5 g	1%
Fiber	1 g	3%
Protein	9 g	

2 to 3 cactus pads (6 to 8 ounces total); or one 8-ounce can nopalitos (cactus pieces), rinsed and drained; or 2 small zucchini, cut into bite-size strips
½ cup chopped onion (1 medium)
½ cup chopped red or green sweet pepper
1 tablespoon margarine or butter
8 eggs
⅓ cup milk
½ teaspoon chili powder
¼ teaspoon salt
Dash ground black pepper
Flour tortillas, warmed (optional)
Salsa (optional)

1. Carefully rinse cactus pads; pat dry. Holding cactus pads with tongs, use a small, sharp knife to carefully trim off eyes around edges and on both sides of pads; discard. Cut cactus pads into thin strips (you should have about 2 cups).

2. In a large skillet cook cactus with onion and sweet pepper in margarine or butter about 3 minutes or until onion is tender.

3. In a bowl beat eggs, milk, chili powder, salt, and black pepper with a fork. Pour egg mixture over vegetables in skillet. Cook over medium heat, without stirring, until mixture begins to set on the bottom and around the edge.

4. Using a spatula or large spoon, lift and fold the partially cooked eggs so the uncooked portion flows underneath. Continue cooking over medium heat about 5 minutes more or until eggs are cooked through, but are still glossy and moist.

5. Remove from heat. If desired, serve with tortillas and salsa. Makes 6 servings.

CACTUS PADS

Nopales, the fleshy, oval pads of the prickly pear cactus, are showing up in many supermarkets. Cooked, they're soft but crunchy, with the slipperiness of okra and flavor of green beans. The pads have tiny, sharp thorns that usually are removed at the market. To remove any thorns, carefully hold the pad and scrape with a paring knife. Use the tip of a sharp knife or a vegetable peeler to remove the thorn bases and any blemishes.

A plate of huevos rancheros is perfect for brunch since it includes four basic food groups— eggs, a bit of cheese, bread in the form of corn tortillas, and vegetables. It is a frequently requested dish throughout Mexico.

ALL MEXICO

*H*uevos Rancheros

MAKES 4 MAIN-DISH SERVINGS   START TO FINISH: 20 MINUTES

NUTRITION FACTS PER SERVING		
		Daily Values
Calories	362	18%
Total fat	24 g	37%
Saturated fat	7 g	36%
Cholesterol	439 mg	146%
Sodium	250 mg	10%
Carbohydrate	18 g	6%
Fiber	1 g	6%
Protein	18 g	

**4 6-inch corn tortillas or 7-inch flour tortillas
2 tablespoons cooking oil
8 eggs
1 tablespoon water
1 cup Ranchero Salsa (see recipe, page 25), warmed
½ cup shredded cheddar cheese or Monterey Jack cheese
Cilantro or parsley sprigs (optional)**

1. Wrap tortillas tightly in foil. Place in a 350° oven about 10 minutes or until heated through.

2. Meanwhile, in a 12-inch skillet heat cooking oil over medium heat. Carefully break eggs into skillet. When whites are set, add water. Cover skillet and cook eggs for 4 to 5 minutes or until the yolks are just firm.

3. Place warm tortillas on dinner plates. Top each with 2 fried eggs. Spoon some of the warm Ranchero Salsa over each. Sprinkle with cheese. If desired, garnish with cilantro or parsley. Serve immediately. Makes 4 main-dish servings.

Rick Strange / The Picture Cube

ALL MEXICO

Tortilla Skillet

CHILAQUILES

Informally translated as "broken up old sombreros," chilaquiles make use of stale corn tortillas. Variations in this quintessential breakfast dish abound in Mexico. Bits of meat and vegetables are stirred into the eggs, as well as any sauce on hand. Serve the dish immediately before the tortillas turn to mush.

MAKES 4 MAIN-DISH SERVINGS   START TO FINISH: 25 MINUTES

6   6-inch corn tortillas
1   tablespoon cooking oil
4   slightly beaten eggs
¼   teaspoon salt
1   recipe Chili Colorado (see page 28) or 2 cups salsa
1½ cups crumbed queso fresco or farmer cheese
½   of a small red onion, sliced and separated into rings

1. Tear tortillas into 1½-inch pieces. Place on an ungreased baking sheet. Bake in a 350° oven for 10 to 12 minutes or until crisp and lightly browned.

2. Heat oil in a large skillet. Add baked tortilla pieces, beaten eggs, and salt. Cook and stir over medium heat until tortillas are coated and eggs are set. Stir in Chili Colorado or salsa and *1 cup* of the cheese. Simmer, uncovered, for 5 minutes.

3. Transfer to a serving dish. Top with remaining cheese and onion rings. Makes 4 main-dish servings.

NUTRITION FACTS PER SERVING		Daily Values
Calories	484	24%
Total fat	25 g	39%
Saturated fat	3 g	13%
Cholesterol	253 mg	84%
Sodium	992 mg	41%
Carbohydrate	41 g	13%
Fiber	12 g	49%
Protein	19 g	

NUTRITION INFORMATION

All of the recipes in this book include a nutrition analysis. You'll find the calorie count and the amount of fat, saturated fat, cholesterol, sodium, carbohydrate, fiber, and protein for each serving. Each of these, except protein, is noted also as a percentage of the Daily Values (dietary standards set by the U.S. Food and Drug Administration).

WHAT YOU NEED

The following dietary guidelines suggest nutrient levels moderately active adults should strive to eat each day. As you change your calorie levels, adjust your fat intake, too. Try to keep the percentage of calories from fat to no more than 30 percent. There's no harm in occasionally going over or

under these guidelines, but the key to good health is maintaining a balanced diet most of the time.

Calories: about 2,000
Total fat: <65 grams
Saturated fat: <20 grams
Cholesterol: <300 milligrams
Sodium: <2,400 milligrams
Carbohydrate: about 300 grams
Dietary fiber: 20 to 30 grams

HOW WE ANALYZE

The Better Homes and Gardens® Test Kitchen computer analyzes each recipe for the nutritional value of a single serving.

■ The analysis does not include optional ingredients.

■ We use the first serving size listed

when a range is given. For example: If we say a recipe "Makes 4 to 6 servings," the Nutrition Facts are based on 4 servings.

■ When ingredient choices (such as margarine or butter) appear in a recipe, we use the first one mentioned for analysis. The ingredient order does not mean we prefer one ingredient over another.

■ When milk is a recipe ingredient, the analysis is calculated using 2-percent milk.

LOW-FAT RECIPES

For recipes that meet our low-fat criteria, a main-dish serving must contain 12 or fewer grams of fat. For side dishes or desserts, the serving must contain 5 or fewer grams of fat.

DESSERTS

ALL MEXICO

flan

Flan was imported directly from Spain. The inverted caramel custard is so well loved it's found on Mexican dessert menus everywhere. Canned milk is traditionally used to give the custard a rich, caramel flavor.

MAKES 6 SERVINGS   PREP: 30 MINUTES   BAKE: 30 MINUTES   CHILL: 4 TO 24 HOURS

⅓ **cup sugar**
3 **beaten eggs**
1 **12-ounce can (1½ cups) evaporated milk**
⅓ **cup sugar**
1 **teaspoon vanilla**
  Fresh fruit (optional)
  Edible flowers (optional)

1. To caramelize sugar, in a heavy skillet cook ⅓ cup sugar over medium-high heat until the sugar begins to melt, shaking skillet occasionally. Do not stir. Once the sugar starts to melt, reduce heat to low and cook about 5 minutes more or until all of the sugar melts and is golden brown, stirring as needed with a wooden spoon.

2. Remove skillet from heat and immediately pour caramelized sugar into an 8-inch flan pan or an 8×1½-inch round baking pan (or divide caramelized sugar among six 6-ounce custard cups). Working quickly, rotate pan or cups so sugar coats the bottom as evenly as possible. Cool.

3. In a medium mixing bowl combine eggs, evaporated milk, ⅓ cup sugar, and vanilla.

4. Place pan or custard cups in a 13×9×2-inch baking pan on an oven rack. Pour egg mixture into pan or custard cups. Pour the hottest tap water available into the 13×9×2-inch baking pan around the flan pan or custard cups to a depth of about ½ inch.

5. Bake in a 325° oven 30 to 35 minutes for pan (35 to 40 minutes for custard cups) or until a knife inserted near the center comes out clean. Immediately remove pan or custard cups from hot water. Cool on a wire rack. Cover and chill for 4 to 24 hours.

6. To unmold flan, loosen edges with a knife, slipping end of knife down sides of pan to let in air. Carefully invert a serving platter over a pan or a dessert plate over a custard cup; turn dishes over together to release custard. Spoon any caramelized sugar that remains in pan on top. If desired, serve with fresh fruit and garnish with edible flowers. Makes 6 servings.

NUTRITION FACTS PER SERVING

		Daily Values
Calories	202	10%
Total fat	7 g	10%
Saturated fat	3 g	16%
Cholesterol	123 mg	40%
Sodium	92 mg	3%
Carbohydrate	28 g	9%
Fiber	0 g	0%
Protein	7 g	

Edible Flowers

Cortez found the indigenous peoples of Mexico using flowers in their cookery for their beauty, taste, and scent—the same reasons we enjoy using them today. Select flowers grown without the use of pesticides or other chemicals. Edible flowers are available in some supermarkets, but the best flowers are unsprayed blossoms from your own garden, including marigolds, pansies, roses, violets, and geraniums.

The economical idea of creating dessert from stale bread came to Mexico via Europe, where bread pudding is featured in several cuisines. Home cooks added cheese, fruits, and nuts depending on what was on hand. Capirotada often is associated with Easter because of the religious symbolism of bread.

ALL MEXICO

Bread Pudding
CAPIROTADA

MAKES 6 TO 8 SERVINGS   PREP: 25 MINUTES   BAKE: 35 MINUTES

NUTRITION FACTS PER SERVING

		Daily Values
Calories	212	10%
Total fat	2 g	3%
Saturated fat	.3 g	1%
Cholesterol	0 mg	0%
Sodium	54 mg	2%
Carbohydrate	47 g	15%
Fiber	3 g	10%
Protein	3 g	

2 **Spindle Rolls* (see recipe, page 17)**
¾ **cup water**
½ **cup packed brown sugar**
3 **inches stick cinnamon**
2 **whole cloves**
2 **apples, peeled, cored, and sliced**
1 **ripe medium plantain or large firm banana, sliced**
⅓ **cup raisins**
¼ **cup coarsely chopped almonds, toasted**
½ **cup shredded asadero, Chihuahua, or Monterey Jack cheese (optional)**
1 **recipe Crema Espesa (see page 91) (optional)**

1. To dry bread, tear Spindle Rolls into small pieces (you should have about 2 cups). Place bread pieces on a baking sheet. Bake in a 350° oven for 8 to 10 minutes or until dried.

2. Meanwhile, for syrup, in a small saucepan combine water, brown sugar, stick cinnamon, and cloves. Bring to boiling. Reduce heat and boil gently, uncovered, for 8 to 10 minutes or until reduced to ¾ cup. Remove the spices with a slotted spoon; discard the spices.

3. In a large bowl toss together dried bread pieces and syrup. Add sliced apples, plantain or banana slices, raisins, and almonds; toss gently. Transfer mixture to an ungreased 2-quart square baking dish.

4. Bake, covered, in a 350° oven for 35 to 40 minutes or until apples are tender. Remove from oven. If desired, sprinkle with cheese and serve with Crema Espesa. Serve warm. Makes 6 to 8 servings.

*Note: French bread may be substituted for the rolls. Choose a firm-textured bread for best results.

ALL MEXICO

Rice Pudding
ARROZ CON LECHE

MAKES 3 CUPS (6 SERVINGS)   PREP: 10 MINUTES   COOK: 20 MINUTES

½ **cup golden raisins**
¼ **cup rum**
3 **cups milk**
½ **cup long-grain rice**
3 **inches stick cinnamon**
¼ **cup sugar**
1 **teaspoon vanilla**
  Ground cinnamon

1. In a small bowl combine the raisins and rum; set aside.

2. In a heavy medium saucepan combine milk, uncooked rice, and stick cinnamon. Bring to boiling. Reduce heat and simmer, covered, about 20 minutes or until rice is tender. Remove stick cinnamon.

3. Drain raisins; discard rum. Stir raisins, sugar, and vanilla into rice mixture. Sprinkle with ground cinnamon. Serve warm or chilled. Makes 3 cups (6 servings).

Rice pudding is a soothing conclusion to a spicy meal. All the basic ingredients needed for this recipe were brought to Mexico from Spain. The creamy rice pudding was flavored with rum or sherry rather than vanilla—a New World product that later became the favorite flavoring agent. Since alcohol was not known in pre-Columbian Mexico, the Spanish introduced the art of distilling rum from molasses, a byproduct of sugar production in the Caribbean Islands.

LOW-FAT

NUTRITION FACTS PER SERVING

		Daily Values
Calories	200	10%
Total fat	3 g	3%
Saturated fat	2 g	7%
Cholesterol	9 mg	3%
Sodium	64 mg	2%
Carbohydrate	38 g	12%
Fiber	.5 g	1%
Protein	6 g	

MEXICAN POT COFFEE

Café de olla, literally coffee from an earthenware pot, is the perfect accompaniment to dessert. Choose a dark-roasted coffee bean and follow the simple directions below. Look for cone-shaped *pilóncillo* (pee-lon-SEE-yoh), unrefined Mexican sugar (shown at left), in Latin American or Mexican specialty stores. Or, substitute dark brown sugar and molasses as noted.

To make Mexican Pot Coffee, in a 3-quart saucepan combine 6 cups *water*, ¼ cup shredded or finely chopped *pilóncillo* or 3 tablespoons packed *dark brown sugar* plus 1 teaspoon *molasses*, 3 inches *stick cinnamon*, and 6 *whole cloves*. Cook and stir over medium heat until pilóncillo is dissolved. Stir in ¾ cup *ground coffee* and bring to boiling. Reduce heat and simmer for 2 minutes. Remove from heat. Cover and let stand for 5 minutes. Strain before serving. Stir in additional *pilóncillo* or *sugar* to taste. Makes 5 (8-ounce) servings.

REGION: TABASCO & YUCATAN PENINSULA

Plantains with Thick Cream
PLÁTANOS CON CREMA

MAKES 4 SERVINGS   START TO FINISH: 25 MINUTES (PLUS 24 HOURS FOR CREMA ESPESA)

2 ripe medium plantains or
   4 firm bananas
3 tablespoons margarine or
   butter
¼ cup packed brown sugar
1 teaspoon vanilla
¼ teaspoon ground cinnamon
2 tablespoons chopped pecans
   or walnuts, or slivered
   almonds, toasted
½ cup Crema Espesa

1. Peel and bias-slice plantains or bananas into ½-inch-thick slices (about 2 cups).

2. Melt margarine or butter in a large skillet. Add plantains or bananas to melted margarine or butter. Heat about 5 minutes for plantains (2 minutes for bananas) or just until warm and tender, gently stirring occasionally. Sprinkle with brown sugar. Stir gently until sugar melts.

3. Carefully stir in vanilla and cinnamon. Sprinkle with nuts. Serve immediately with Crema Espesa. Makes 4 servings.

CREMA ESPESA

In a small saucepan heat 1 cup *whipping cream* (not ultra-pasteurized) over low heat until warm (90° to 100°). Pour the cream into a small bowl. Stir in 2 tablespoons *buttermilk.* Cover and let the mixture stand at room temperature for 24 to 30 hours (do not stir) or until mixture is thickened. Store in a covered container in the refrigerator for up to a week. Stir before serving. Makes 1 cup.

The plantain—a tropical fruit resembling a banana with thick, green skin—must be cooked to be enjoyed. The skin will turn almost black when fully ripened at room temperature. Prepare the recipe for Crema Espesa a few days in advance. Its slight tang is a wonderful counterpoint to the dessert's sweetness. If you don't have time to make the thick cream, substitute crème fraîche or a bit of sour cream or whipped cream.

NUTRITION FACTS
PER SERVING WITH
2 TABLESPOONS CREMA ESPESA

		Daily Values
Calories	358	17%
Total fat	22 g	34%
Saturated fat	9 g	43%
Cholesterol	41 mg	13%
Sodium	123 mg	5%
Carbohydrate	41 g	13%
Fiber	2 g	9%
Protein	2 g	

*These well-known
shortbread cookies go by
the Spanish word for dust,
most likely because they're
always dusted with
powdered sugar. The
recipe came to Mexico
with the Spanish, but the
cookies have come to be
known as Mexican
wedding cakes in the
United States—perhaps
because almonds
symbolize happiness.*

ALL MEXICO

Mexican Shortbread Cookies
POLVORONES

MAKES 48 COOKIES   PREP: 30 MINUTES   COOK: 20 MINUTES PER BATCH

NUTRITION FACTS PER COOKIE

		Daily Values
Calories	67	3%
Total fat	4 g	6%
Saturated fat	2 g	12%
Cholesterol	10 mg	3%
Sodium	39 mg	1%
Carbohydrate	7 g	2%
Fiber	0 g	0%
Protein	1 g	

1 cup butter
½ cup sifted powdered sugar
1 tablespoon water
1 teaspoon vanilla
2 cups all-purpose flour
½ cup ground toasted almonds
**¼ teaspoon ground cinnamon
    or 2 teaspoons finely
    shredded orange peel**
**¾ to 1 cup sifted powdered
    sugar**

1. In a medium mixing bowl beat butter with an electric mixer on medium to high speed for 30 seconds. Add the ½ cup powdered sugar and beat until fluffy. Beat in the water and vanilla until combined. Beat in as much of the flour as you can with the mixer. Stir in any remaining flour, almonds, and cinnamon or orange peel. If necessary, chill the dough for 1 hour or until easy to handle.

2. Shape dough into 1-inch balls. Place on an ungreased cookie sheet.

3. Bake in a 325° oven about 20 minutes or until bottoms are lightly browned. Cool cookies on a wire rack. Gently shake cooled cookies, a few at a time, in a plastic bag with the ¾ to 1 cup powdered sugar. Makes 48 cookies.

MAKE AHEAD

Prepare and bake the cookies as directed, except don't shake the cookies in powdered sugar. Place in a freezer container or bag and freeze for up to 1 month. To serve, thaw cookies for 15 minutes. Shake cookies in powdered sugar.

Jeff Greenberg / The Picture Cube

REGION: OAXACA

Buñuelos

MAKES 24 BUÑUELOS   PREP: 1 HOUR   FRY: 2 MINUTES PER BATCH

2 cups all-purpose flour
1 teaspoon baking powder
½ teaspoon salt
¼ teaspoon cream of tartar
2 tablespoons shortening
2 beaten eggs
⅓ cup milk
  Cooking oil for frying
1 recipe Brown Sugar Syrup or
  1 recipe Cinnamon Sugar

1. In a large mixing bowl combine flour, baking powder, salt, and cream of tartar. Cut in shortening until mixture resembles coarse crumbs. Make a well in the center of the dry ingredients.

2. In a small mixing bowl combine eggs and milk. Add to flour mixture all at once. Stir just until dough clings together.

3. On a lightly floured surface knead dough about 2 minutes or until soft and smooth. Divide dough into 24 equal portions. Shape each portion into a ball. Cover dough and let rest for 15 minutes.

4. In a heavy 10-inch skillet heat about ¾ inch of cooking oil to 375°. Meanwhile, on a lightly floured surface roll each ball to a 4-inch circle. Fry dough circles in hot oil about 1 minute on each side or until golden brown. Drain on paper towels. Keep warm in a 300° oven while frying remaining dough. Drizzle with Brown Sugar Syrup or sprinkle with Cinnamon Sugar. Makes 24 buñuelos.

BROWN SUGAR SYRUP

In a small saucepan combine 1 cup packed *dark brown sugar* and ½ cup *water*. Cook and stir over medium-high heat until sugar dissolves. Add 3 inches *stick cinnamon* or dash *ground cinnamon*. Bring to boiling. Reduce heat and simmer, uncovered, for 5 minutes. Remove from heat. Stir in ½ teaspoon *vanilla*. Discard cinnamon stick. Serve warm. Makes ¾ cup syrup.

CINNAMON SUGAR

Stir together ½ cup *granulated sugar* and 1 teaspoon *ground cinnamon*. Sprinkle over warm buñuelos.

The Spaniards probably brought these traditional Christmas fritters to Mexico. Served with a coating of cinnamon sugar or coated in cinnamon syrup, these sweet treats will turn any occasion into a feast day. In Oaxaca, it's said the buñuelos (boon-WAY-lohs) are served in pottery containers that are broken as the last fritters are eaten, to ensure good luck in the days ahead.

NUTRITION FACTS PER BUÑUELOS
WITH BROWN SUGAR SYRUP

		Daily Values
Calories	121	6%
Total fat	6 g	9%
Saturated fat	1 g	5%
Cholesterol	18 mg	5%
Sodium	69 mg	2%
Carbohydrate	15 g	4%
Fiber	.3 g	1%
Protein	2 g	

MAKE AHEAD

Prepare and fry buñuelos as directed, except don't drizzle with syrup or sprinkle with sugar. Place in a freezer container or bag and freeze for up to 2 months. To serve, place frozen buñuelos on a large baking sheet and cover loosely with foil. Heat in a 350° oven about 15 minutes or until heated through. Serve as directed.

Index

Page numbers in bold indicate photographs.

A – C

Appetizers. *See also* Salsas
    Appetizer Tarts, **6,** 8
    Empanadas with Chicken
        Picadillo, **6,** 7
    Peanuts, Deviled, 9
    Pepitas, Deviled, 9
    Quesadillas, 10, **11**
    White Bean Dip, 12 LOW-FAT
Avocados
    Avocado Soup, 37
    Guacamole, 22
Banana Leaves, Chicken Baked in,
    50, 51 LOW-FAT
Beans
    Appetizer Tarts (with bean
        filling), **6,** 8
    Bean Burritos, 76, **77**
    Black and White Beans with
        Sweet Peppers, 79 LOW-FAT
    Black Bean Soup, 80 LOW-FAT
    Crab and White Bean
        Chowder, 68 LOW-FAT
    Flautas, 56
    Rice and Beans, Oaxacan, 78 LOW-FAT
    White Bean Dip, 12 LOW-FAT
Beef
    Beef Stew in a Pot, 42, **43**
    Chimichangas, 40
    Fajitas, **38,** 39
    Meatball Soup, 41 LOW-FAT
Beverages
    Cinnamon Hot Chocolate, 13
    Coffee, Mexican Pot, 89
    hot chocolate the easy way, 13
    Margaritas, 14 NO-FAT
    Sangria, 14 NO-FAT
    Water, Jamaica Flower, 15 NO-FAT
Bread
    Bread of the Dead, **16,** 18
    Bread Pudding, 88 LOW-FAT
    Rolls, Spindle, **16,** 17 NO-FAT
    Three Kings' Bread, 19
Buñuelos, 93

Burritos, Bean 76, **77**
Cactus pads
    cactus pads, 82
    Eggs with Cactus, Scrambled,
        82, **83**
Chayote
    chayote, 31
    Chayote Salad, **30,** 31 LOW-FAT
    Corn- and Pepper-Stuffed
        Chayote, 36 LOW-FAT
Cheese
    Mexican cheeses, 48
    Potato- and Cheese-Stuffed Chili
        Peppers, 34, **35** LOW-FAT
    Seafood Enchiladas, 69
Chicken
    Appetizer Tarts (with chicken
        filling), **6,** 8
    Chicken and Lime Soup,
        58, 59 LOW-FAT
    Chicken and Rice, 61
    Chicken Baked in Banana
        Leaves, **50,** 51 LOW-FAT
    Chicken Picadillo, **6,** 7
    Chicken with Green Pumpkin
        Seed Mole, 54, **55** LOW-FAT
    Chicken with Mole, 52
    Chicken with New Mexican-Style
        Rub, 57 LOW-FAT
    Enchiladas, Swiss, 53
    Flautas, 56
    Quesadillas, 10, **11**
    Soup, Dry, **72,** 73
    Stew, Tablecloth-Stainer, 60
Chili peppers (see Peppers, chili)
Chimichangas, 40
Chipotle Chili Salsa, 27
Chocolate
    Cinnamon Hot Chocolate, 13
    hot chocolate the easy way, 13
    Chowder, Crab and White
        Bean, 68 LOW-FAT
Cilantro
    cilantro, 73
    Shrimp in Cilantro Sauce,
        70, **71** LOW-FAT
Coffee, Mexican Pot, 89
Cookies, Mexican Shortbread, 92

Corn- and Pepper-Stuffed
    Chayote, 36 LOW-FAT
Crab and White Bean
    Chowder, 68 LOW-FAT

D – L

Desserts
    Bread Pudding, 88 LOW-FAT
    Buñuelos, 93
    Crema Espesa, **90,** 91
    Flan, **86,** 87
    Plantains with Thick Cream,
        90, 91
    Rice Pudding, 89 LOW-FAT
    Shortbread Cookies, Mexican, 92
Egg dishes
    Huevos Rancheros, 84
    Scrambled Eggs with Cactus,
        82, **83**
    Tortilla Skillet, 85
Enchiladas
    Seafood Enchiladas, 69
    Swiss Enchiladas, 53
Fajitas, **38,** 39
Fish and shellfish. *See also* Shrimp
    Crab and White Bean
        Chowder, 68 LOW-FAT
    Drunken Fish, 64 LOW-FAT
    Fish in Smoked Pepper
        Marinade, 65 LOW-FAT
    Fish Tacos, 66, **67** LOW-FAT
    Seafood Enchiladas, 69
    Snapper Veracruz, **62,** 63 LOW-FAT
Flan, **86,** 87
Flautas, 56
Flowers, edible, 87
Fruit. *See also* specific kinds of fruit
    Bread Pudding, 88 LOW-FAT
    Christmas Eve Salad, 33
    Stew, Tablecloth-Stainer, 60
Guacamole, 22
Huevos Rancheros, 84
Jicama
    jicama, 32
    Jicama Pico de Gallo Salad, 32
Lentil Soup, 81 LOW-FAT
Lime Soup, Chicken and,
    58, 59 LOW-FAT

M – S

Mangoes
  mangoes, 29
  Mango Salsa, 29 NO-FAT
Margaritas, 14 NO-FAT
Meatball Soup, 41 LOW-FAT
Moles
  Chicken with Green Pumpkin
    Seed Mole, 54, **55** LOW-FAT
  Chicken with Mole, 52
Nutrition information, 85
Peanuts, Deviled, 9
Peppers, Black and White Beans
    with Sweet, 79 LOW-FAT
Peppers, chili
  Chili Colorado, 28
  Chipotle Chili Salsa, 27
  Corn- and Pepper-Stuffed
    Chayote, 36 LOW-FAT
  Fish in Smoked Pepper
    Marinade, 65 LOW-FAT
  Poblano Rice with Vegetables,
    75 LOW-FAT
  Potato- and Cheese-Stuffed Chili
    Peppers, 34, **35** LOW-FAT
  Stuffed Chilies in Walnut Sauce,
    46, **47**
Picante Sauce, 24 NO-FAT
Plantains with Thick Cream, **90,** 91
Pork
  Chilies in Walnut Sauce, Stuffed,
    46, **47**
  Pork Chops in Adobo Sauce, 49
    LOW-FAT
  Shredded Savory Pork, 45
  Stew, Tablecloth-Stainer, 60
  Tacos, Shredded Pork, 48
  Tamales, Shredded Pork, 44
Potatoes
  Beef Stew in a Pot, 42, **43**
  Meatball Soup, 41 LOW-FAT
  Potato- and Cheese-Stuffed Chili
    Peppers, 34, **35** LOW-FAT
Pudding
  Bread Pudding, 88 LOW-FAT
  Rice Pudding, 89 LOW-FAT
Pumpkin seeds
  Chicken with Green Pumpkin
    Seed Mole, 54, **55** LOW-FAT
  Pepitas, Deviled, 9

Quesadillas, 10, **11**
Rice
  Chicken and Rice, 61
  Drunken Fish, 64 LOW-FAT
  Mexican Rice, 74 LOW-FAT
  Oaxacan Rice and Beans, 78 LOW-FAT
  Poblano Rice with Vegetables,
    75 LOW-FAT
  Rice Pudding, 89 LOW-FAT
  Shrimp in Cilantro Sauce,
    70, **71** LOW-FAT
  Soup, Dry, **72,** 73
Rolls, Spindle, **16, 17** NO-FAT
Salads
  Chayote Salad, **30,** 31 LOW-FAT
  Christmas Eve Salad, 33
  Jicama Pico de Gallo Salad, 32
Salsas
  Chipotle Chili Salsa, 27
  Guacamole, 22
  Mango Salsa, 29 NO-FAT
  Picante Sauce, 24 NO-FAT
  Ranchero Salsa, 25
  Salsa Verde, 26 NO-FAT
  Tomato Salsa, Fresh, 23 NO-FAT
Sangria, 14 NO-FAT
Sauces
  Adobo Sauce, Pork Chops in,
    49 LOW-FAT
  Chili Colorado, 28
  Cilantro Sauce, Shrimp in,
    70, **71** LOW-FAT
  Green Pumpkin Seed Mole,
    Chicken with, 54, **55** LOW-FAT
  Mole, Chicken with, 52
  Walnut Sauce, 46, **47**
Shortbread Cookies, Mexican, 92
Shrimp
  Seafood Enchiladas, 69
  Shrimp in Cilantro Sauce,
    70, **71** LOW-FAT
Snapper Veracruz, **62,** 63 LOW-FAT
Soups and stews
  Avocado Soup, 37
  Beef Stew in a Pot, 42, **43**
  Black Bean Soup, 80 LOW-FAT
  Chicken and Lime Soup,
    58, 59 LOW-FAT
  Crab and White Bean Chowder,
    68 LOW-FAT
  Dry Soup, **72,** 73

Lentil Soup, 81 LOW-FAT
Meatball Soup, 41 LOW-FAT
Tablecloth-Stainer Stew, 60
Spinach Tortillas, 20

T – Z

Tacos
  Fish Tacos, 66, **67** LOW-FAT
  Pork Tacos, Shredded, 48
Tamales, Shredded Pork, 44
Tomatillos
  Chicken with Green Pumpkin
    Seed Mole, 54, **55** LOW-FAT
  Chipotle Chili Salsa, 27
  Enchiladas, Swiss, 53
  Salsa Verde, 26 NO-FAT
  tomatillos, 70
Tomatoes
  Beef Stew in a Pot, 42, **43**
  Fish, Drunken, 64 LOW-FAT
  Salsa, Fresh Tomato, 23 NO-FAT
  Salsa, Ranchero, 25
  Sauce, Picante, 24 NO-FAT
  Snapper Veracruz, **62,** 63 LOW-FAT
Tortillas
  Bean Burritos, 76, **77**
  Chicken and Lime Soup,
    58, 59 LOW-FAT
  Chili Powder Tortillas, 20
  Chimichangas, 40
  Corn Tortillas, 21
  Enchiladas, Swiss, 53
  Fajitas, **38,** 39
  Fish Tacos, 66, **67** LOW-FAT
  Flautas, 56
  Flour Tortillas, 20
  Huevos Rancheros, 84
  Pork Tacos, Shredded, 48
  Seafood Enchiladas, 69
  Spinach Tortillas, 20
  Tortilla Skillet, 85
  Tostaditas, 12
Vegetables. *See also* specific kinds
    of vegetables
  Beef Stew in a Pot, 42, **43**
  Christmas Eve Salad, 33
  Meatball Soup, 41 LOW-FAT
  Poblano Rice with Vegetables,
    75 LOW-FAT
  Rice, Mexican, 74 LOW-FAT

Metric Cooking Hints

By making a few conversions, cooks in Australia, Canada, and the United Kingdom can use the recipes in *Better Homes and Gardens® Mexican Cooking* with confidence. The charts on this page provide a guide for converting measurements from the U.S. customary system, which is used throughout this book, to the imperial and metric systems. The conversion table for oven temperatures accommodates the differences in oven calibrations.

Product Differences: Most of the ingredients called for in the recipes in this book are available in English-speaking countries. However, some are known by different names. Here are some common American ingredients and their possible counterparts:
■ Sugar is granulated or castor sugar.
■ Powdered sugar is icing sugar.
■ All-purpose flour is plain household flour or white flour. When self-rising flour is used in place of all-purpose flour in a recipe that calls for leavening, omit the leavening agent (baking soda or baking powder) and salt.
■ Light-colored corn syrup is golden syrup.
■ Cornstarch is cornflour.
■ Baking soda is bicarbonate of soda.
■ Vanilla is vanilla essence.
■ Green, red, and yellow sweet peppers are capsicums.
■ Golden raisins are sultanas.

Volume and Weight: Americans traditionally use cup measures for liquid and solid ingredients. The chart at top right shows the approximate imperial and metric equivalents. If you are accustomed to weighing solid ingredients, the following approximate equivalents will be helpful.
■ 1 cup butter, castor sugar, or rice = 8 ounces = about 250 grams
■ 1 cup flour = 4 ounces = about 125 grams
■ 1 cup icing sugar = 5 ounces = about 150 grams
Spoon measures are used for smaller amounts of ingredients. Although the size of the tablespoon varies slightly in different countries, for practical purposes and for recipes in this book, a straight substitution is all that's necessary.

Measurements made using cups or spoons always should be level unless stated otherwise.

Equivalents: U.S. = Australia/U.K.

⅛ teaspoon = 0.5 millilitre
¼ teaspoon = 1 millilitre
½ teaspoon = 2 millilitres
1 teaspoon = 5 millilitres
1 tablespoon = 1 tablespoon
¼ cup = 2 tablespoons = 2 fluid ounces = 60 millilitres
⅓ cup = ¼ cup = 3 fluid ounces = 90 millilitres
½ cup = ⅓ cup = 4 fluid ounces = 120 millilitres
⅔ cup = ½ cup = 5 fluid ounces = 150 millilitres
¾ cup = ⅔ cup = 6 fluid ounces = 180 millilitres
1 cup = ¾ cup = 8 fluid ounces = 240 millilitres
1¼ cups = 1 cup
2 cups = 1 pint
1 quart = 1 litre
½ inch = 1.27 centimetres
1 inch = 2.54 centimetres

Baking Pan Sizes

American	Metric
8×1½-inch round baking pan	20×4-centimetre cake tin
9×1½-inch round baking pan	23×3.5-centimetre cake tin
11×7×1½-inch baking pan	28×18×4-centimetre baking tin
13×9×2-inch baking pan	30×20×3-centimetre baking tin
2-quart rectangular baking dish	30×20×3-centimetre baking tin
15×10×2-inch baking pan	30×25×2-centimetre baking tin (Swiss roll tin)
9-inch pie plate	22×4- or 23×4-centimetre pie plate
7- or 8-inch springform pan	18- or 20-centimetre springform or loose-bottom cake tin
9×5×3-inch loaf pan	23×13×7-centimetre or 2-pound narrow loaf tin or paté tin
1½-quart casserole	1.5-litre casserole
2-quart casserole	2-litre casserole

Oven Temperature Equivalents

Fahrenheit Setting	Celsius Setting*	Gas Setting
300°F	150°C	Gas Mark 2 (slow)
325°F	160°C	Gas Mark 3 (moderately slow)
350°F	180°C	Gas Mark 4 (moderate)
375°F	190°C	Gas Mark 5 (moderately hot)
400°F	200°C	Gas Mark 6 (hot)
425°F	220°C	Gas Mark 7
450°F	230°C	Gas Mark 8 (very hot)
Broil		Grill

* Electric and gas ovens may be calibrated using Celsius. However, for an electric oven, increase the Celsius setting 10° to 20° when cooking above 160°C. For convection or forced-air ovens (gas or electric), lower the temperature setting 10°C when cooking at all heat levels.